Elisabeth M---

First German Reader (Volume 3)
bilingual for speakers of English

Elementary Level

LANGUAGE
PRACTICE
PUBLISHING

We strive to avoid typos and inaccuracies. However, on occasion we make mistakes. We value your contributions and help in correcting them. To report typos or inaccuracies, please mail to editor@lppbooks.com
Copyright © 2013 by Language Practice Publishing
All rights reserved. This book is in copyright.

Inhaltsverzeichnis

Kapitel 1 Verständigungsprobleme 4
Kapitel 2 Ein Lädiertes Kleid 7
Kapitel 3 Flucht in Dunkler Nacht 10
Kapitel 4 Ein Japanischer Vertrag 13
Kapitel 5 Liebe auf den Ersten Blick 15
Kapitel 6 Fußball 19
Kapitel 7 Eine Verfolgungsjagd 21
Kapitel 8 Ein Schlechtes Horoskop 23
Kapitel 9 Ein Sehr Dringender Anruf 25
Kapitel 10 Die Gäste 27
Kapitel 11 Ein Unglücklicher Raubüberfall 30
Kapitel 12 Ein Ausgestopftes Tier 33
Kapitel 13 Eine Tolle Party 35
Kapitel 14 Eine Mysteriöse Stimme 37
Kapitel 15 Eine Seltsame Gruppe 39
Kapitel 16 Ein Wissenschaftliches Experiment 41
Kapitel 17 Ein Unvorhersehbares Detail 43
Kapitel 18 Aberglauben 46
Kapitel 19 Gute Nachbarn 48
Kapitel 20 Ein Ruheloser Patient 50
Kapitel 21 Ein Vorfall am See 52
Kapitel 22 Eine Kaffee-Garantie 54
Kapitel 23 Ein Zotteliger Partner 56
Kapitel 24 Die Beste Kaffeemaschine auf der Welt 58
Kapitel 25 Wer Braucht es Mehr? 60
Kapitel 26 Ein Fataler Streit 63
Kapitel 27 Ein Guter Alter Freund 65
Kapitel 28 Maulwürfe - Musikliebhaber 67
Kapitel 29 Kriminalpsychologie 69
Buchtipps 71

1

Verständigungsprobleme

Sobald David und Robert ihren College-Abschluss hatten, beschlossen sie, bei der Polizei zu arbeiten. Sie dachten daran, wie interessant es gewesen war, die Polizeipatrouille zu begleiten und anschließend Berichte für die Straftaten-Kolumne zu schreiben. Das hatte sie sehr beeinflusst. Und David hatte bald Glück. Er wurde in die Polizeieinheit aufgenommen. Robert hatte nicht soviel Glück, da er Deutscher war. Aber Robert fand es sehr interessant, die Verbrechen zu untersuchen; darum wurde er Privatdetektiv.
Ein Ausländer hatte vor, eine Bank zu überfallen. Er bereitete sich gründlich vor, betrat das Gebäude und ging zum Kassenschalter. Sein Plan war, so wenig Aufmerksamkeit wie möglich erregen. Er bedeckte seine Plastikpistole mit seinem Hut, den er auf die Ablage vor dem Schalter legte. Dann wartete er, bis die Bankangestellte ihn

Some Difficulties with Translation

As soon as David and Robert finished their studies at college they decided to work for the Police. They both remembered how it was interesting to accompany the Police patrol and then to write reports for the criminal column. All that has influenced them a lot. And soon David was lucky. He was accepted to the Police crew. Robert was not lucky as he was a German citizen. But Robert understood that it was very interesting for him to investigate the crimes. That's why he became a private detective. Once a foreigner was going to robber a bank. He prepared thoroughly, entered the building and came up to the cashier window. He planned to attract as little attention as possible. He covered his plastic gun with his hat which he placed on the stand in front of the window. Then he waited till the cashier greeted him politely. And then he gave her a note. It said the following: «it's a robbery. I

höflich begrüßte. Er gab ihr einen Zettel auf dem folgendes stand: «Dies ist ein Überfall. Ich habe eine Pistole unter meinem Hut, die direkt auf Sie zeigt. Legen Sie schnell alles Geld in die Tüte und lassen Sie es niemanden merken.»

Die Kassiererin nahm den Zettel und las ihn aufmerksam. Ihre Miene änderte sich nicht – sie blieb freundlich. Sie schaute eine Weile auf den Zettel, drehte ihn dann hin und her und fragte: «Wie kann ich Ihnen helfen?»

Der Bankräuber zeigte irritiert auf den Zettel. «Ja, aber ich kann kein Wort entziffern,» sagte die Angestellte. «Sie haben eine unleserliche Handschrift.»

Um ehrlich zu sein – die Nachricht bestand aus einem schrecklichen Gekritzel. Sie verstand wirklich nicht, was da stand. Deshalb blieb die Frau hinter dem Schalter weiter freundlich. Sie konnte überhaupt nicht verstehen, was er wollte.

Der Bankräuber wurde nervös. Er versuchte, seine Absicht zu erklären, sprach aber kaum Englisch. Und sie verstand seine Mischung aus Spanisch und Englisch noch weniger als die Worte auf dem Zettel. Der Bankräuber erklärte es ihr erneut, mit demselben Ergebnis. Hinter ihm warteten einige Leute und schließlich ging er irritiert davon.

Die nächste Person in der Warteschlange war Robert. Er reichte der Angestellten wichtige Quittungen und wartete, bis sie alle bearbeitet hatte. Plötzlich wurde er auf einen seltsamen Zettel aufmerksam, der auf der Ablage lag. Der Bankräuber war so nervös gewesen, dass er seine Nachricht liegenließ!

Und da Robert Privatdetektiv war, konnte er mit der Nachricht mehr anfangen als die Bankangestellte. Die Schrift war wirklich furchtbar; es war nur Gekritzel! Aber er brauchte nur eine halbe Minute um zu entziffern was da stand.

Woher haben Sie das?» fragte Robert die Angestellte. Sie erklärte es ihm. Robert sah sie eindringlich an.

have a gun under my hat and it's pointed right at you. Quickly put all the money into the package and don't attract any attention.»

The cashier took the note and began to read it attentively. Her expression did not change - it was as friendly as it was before. She looked at the note long enough. Then she twiddled it and asked:

«So how can I help you?»

The robber pointed irritatingly with his finger at the note.

«Yes, but I can't understand a word here," said the cashier. «You have a very illegible writing».

To tell the truth - there were awful scribbles on the note. And she really couldn't understand what was written there. That's why the woman in the window continued to smile in a friendly way. And she didn't understand at all what he wanted.

The robber became nervous. He tried to explain her his intention. But he couldn't speak almost any English. And she understood from his mixture of Spanish and English even less than from the note. The robber explained it all to her once more, but the result was the same. A small queue began to gather behind him, and he went away in irritation.

It happened so that the next person in the queue was Robert. He handed the cashier necessary receipts and waited till she did all the required operations. And suddenly his attention was attracted by a strange note that was lying on the stand. The robber was so nervous that he forgot to take away his note! And as Robert worked as a private detective, he dealt with the message better than the cashier. The writing was really very awful; there were just scribbles! But just in half a minute he understood all that was written there.

«Where did you get it?» Robert asked the cashier. She explained it to him. Robert looked at her very attentively.

«Wir müssen die Polizei rufen,» sagte Robert. «Die Verständigungsprobleme haben Sie gerade vor einem Überfall bewahrt.»

«We have to call the Police,» said Robert. «Difficulties with translation have just saved you from the real robbery.»

2

Ein Lädiertes Kleid

Roberts Ehefrau Lena besaß eine chemische Reinigung. Sie hatte ihren Job immer gemocht. Aber in letzter Zeit life es nicht gut. Lena war sehr aufgebracht. In ihrer Straße mussten einige große Läden zumachen und es kamen nur selten Kunden. Und nun kam den ganzen Tag niemand in die Reinigung. Lena erkannte, dass sie ihr Geschäft bald aufgeben musste und es machte ihr Angst, da ihr Armut und Arbeitslosigkeit drohten.

Da kam ein neuer Kunde in die Reinigung. Der Mann brachte ein blaues Abendkleid zum Reinigen. Es war nicht neu aber sehr hübsch und definitiv sehr teuer. Lena freute sich über den Auftrag. Doch sie wusste, es würde ihre chemische Reinigung nicht retten. Dann passierte etwas Furchtbares!

Sie ruinierte das Kleid während des Reinigungsvorganges! Das war ihr noch nie passiert. Das Kleid sah nach der chemischen

A Damaged Dress

Robert's wife Lena was the owner of a dry-cleaner's. She always liked to do this job. But lately the work was going badly. Lena was very upset. A few big shops closed in their street and the clients appeared very rarely. And now no one visited the dry cleaner's during the whole day. Lena understood that she would have to close the business soon, and she was terrified because of this, as it threatened her with poverty and unemployment.

Once a new client appeared in the dry cleaner's. The man brought blue evening dress to clean. It was not new but beautiful and definitely very expensive. Lena was glad to get this order. Though she understood that it wouldn't save her dry cleaner's. And some awful thing happened! During the dry cleaning she totally spoiled the dress! It never happened to her before.

Reinigung einfach furchtbar aus. In dem Zustand konnte sie es dem Besitzer nicht zurückgeben. «Was mache ich jetzt?» fragte Lena Robert traurig. «Kaufe dasselbe Kleid. Ich sehe keine andere Lösung in dieser Situation,» war Roberts Rat.
Lena hörte ihm zu und war einverstanden, dasselbe Kleid zu kaufen. Sie ging in fast alle Kleiderläden in der Stadt, doch keiner hatte dieses Kleid. Inzwischen war es Zeit, dem Kunden das Kleid zurückzugeben. Lena geriet in Panik.
Sie war sehr müde und das Problem regte sie sehr auf. Wie durch ein Wunder fand sie am Abend ein Kleid, das genauso aussah. Es kostete ein Vermögen, aber es gab keine andere Lösung und Lena musste das Kleid kaufen.
Der Kunde holte das Kleid am Morgen ab. Er bemerkte nichts, dankte Lena und ging weg. Lena und Robert waren erleichtert.
Am nächsten Tag entschied Lena, ihrer Assistentin zu sagen, dass die Reinigung zumachen würde und sie sich nach einer neuen Stelle umsehen musste. Es war schwer, darüber nachzudenken, doch es gab keine andere Möglichkeit. Doch dann änderte sich plötzlich alles. Als erstes kam eine ältere Frau mit einem Mantel in die Reinigung, dann ein Mann mit ein paar Anzügen, dann brachte eine Frau ein paar Blusen und Kleider. Lena traute ihren Augen nicht! Ein Kunde nach dem anderen betrat die Reinigung. Am Abend sagte Lena ihrer Assistentin nichts über die Schließung. Sie beschloss, zu warten.
Und sie war sehr erstaunt. Auch am folgenden Tag kamen Kunden. Lena verstand nicht, was da passierte. Aber dann sprach sie mit einem der Kunden und erfuhr den Grund.
«Wissen Sie, mir wurde gesagt, Ihre Reinigung ist die beste in der Stadt,» sagte der Kunde. «Der Mann meiner Freundin brachte ihr blaues Konzertkleid hierher. Das Kleid ist über 10 Jahre alt. Und meine Freundin sagte mir, dass es nach der Reinigung bei Ihnen wie neu

The dress looked awful after the dry cleaning. She could not return it to the owner in such an awful condition.
«And what do I do now?» Lena asked Robert sadly
«Buy the same dress. I can't see another way out of this situation,» Robert advised her.
Lena listened to him and agreed to buy the same dress. She visited almost all the shops in the city but there was no such dress. Meanwhile it was time to return the order to the client. Lena panicked a lot. She was very tired and upset because of this problem. She miraculously found such a dress only in the evening. It cost a fortune, but there was no another way out and Lena had to buy it. In the morning the client got his order. He didn't suspect anything, thanked Lena and went away. Lena and Robert felt relieved.
The next day Lena decided to tell her assistant that the dry cleaner's was going to be closed and she would have to look for a new job. It was hard to think about that but there was no other way out. However, suddenly everything has changed. First, an old woman came to the dry cleaner's with a coat, then a man with a few suits, then a woman brought a few blouses and dresses. Lena could not believe her eyes! One client after another came to the dry cleaner's. That evening Lena told her assistant nothing about the closing. She decided to wait. And she was very surprised. The next day clients kept on coming. Lena couldn't understand what was happening. But once she spoke with one of the visitors and got to know the reason.
«You know, I was told that you have the best dry cleaner's in the city», the client told her. «My friend's husband brought here her blue concert dress. The dress was about 10 years old. And now my friend says that after your dry cleaner's it looks like new! And I saw it myself - it's true!»

aussieht! Und ich habe es selbst gesehen – es stimmt!
Lena verstand, was passiert war. Es ging natürlich um dieses Kleid! Seitdem hatte die chemische Reinigung immer viele Aufträge.

Then Lena understood what had happened. Of course it was the same dress! Since that time there were always a lot of orders at the dry cleaner's.

3

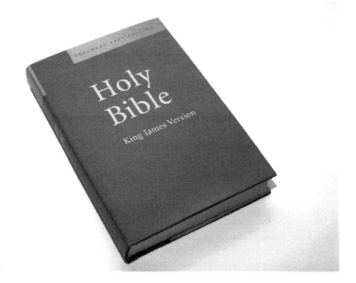

Flucht in Dunkler Nacht

Ron war lange Zeit ein erfolgreicher Räuber gewesen. Doch dann wurde er ein gewöhnlicher Gefangener. Natürlich war er nicht begeistert über die Wende in seiner «Karriere». Nach nur zwei Monaten im Gefängnis gelang es ihm nicht nur, sich einen Fluchtplan auszudenken, er koordinierte auch alles mit seinen zahlreichen Komplizen. Sie besuchten ihn mehrmals im Gefängnis und koordinierten dabei alles heimlich. Dann war der Tag der Flucht endlich da. Ron war gutgelaunt. Er wartete bis es Nacht war und war zur vereinbarten Zeit fertig. Er machte ein Seil aus mehreren Bett-Tüchern. Dann ließ er es durch die Gitterstäbe am Fenster nach unten. Die Überwachungskamera befand sich im vierten Stock, daher musste er sein Bestes geben. Die Nacht war völlig dunkel. Robert hoffte, dass das Seil und seine Komplizen unbemerkt bleiben würden. Er wartete ein paar Minuten. Dann fing er an, sich Sorgen zu machen. Dann erhielt er von unten ein Zeichen

The Dark Night's Escape

Ron has been a successful robber for a long time. But then he became an ordinary prisoner. Of course, he did not like such turn in his career. After just two month in prison, he managed not only to think up a plan of escape, but he also coordinated everything with his partners in crime who were at large. They visited him in prison several times and during these meetings they coordinated everything on the sly. And finally the day of the escape came. Ron was in a good mood. He waited for the night to come and at the appointed time he was ready. He made a rope out of several sheets. Then he lowered it down out of the window through the bars. The camera was situated on the fourth floor so he had to do his best. The night was absolutely dark. Ron hoped that the rope and his partners in crime would not be noticed. He waited for a few minutes. And then he began to worry. Then he received a signal from below - someone

– jemand zog dreimal an dem Seil. Es war das Zeichen, das sie vereinbart hatten. Es bedeutete, alles war bereit. Ron war sehr froh und begann, das Seil einzuziehen. Er brauchte nicht lange. Bald zog er ein großes Bündel durch die Stäbe ins Zimmer.

«Exzellent!» flüsterte er.

Er hatte seine Komplizen gebeten, eine geladene Waffe in das Paket zu legen. Ron hatte vor, sie gegen die Wärter zu benutzen. Er hoffte, mit der Waffe die Wärter dazu zu bringen, die Tür zu öffnen. Ron begann, das Paket auszuwickeln. Doch es war mit Packpapier und Klebeband mehrlagig umwickelt. «Idioten! – dachte Ron. – Das ist kein Weihnachtsgeschenk. Was haben die nur gedacht?» Er war sauer. In seiner Zelle gab es weder Schere noch Messer. Er hatte wenig Zeit. Das Klebeband machte ein lautes Geräusch als Ron anfing, das Paket auszuwickeln. Ron befürchtete, dass die Wärter das Geräusch hören könnten. Er versuchte, das Klebeband geräuschlos Schicht für Schicht zu lösen. Es dauerte vierzig Minuten. Die Dummheit seiner Komplizen verfluchend, kam Ron endlich an das Papier. Er fing an, es zu lösen. Endlich sah er darunter die Schachtel. «Verpackt wie im Laden,» – flüsterte Ron ärgerlich.

Aber nach genauer Untersuchung der Schachtel schien es Ron, dass alles noch viel schlimmer war. Es war nicht die Schachtel mit der Waffe, es war ... eine Bibel.

Ron saß eine Minute lang nur da und schaute auf das Buch. Er verstand gar nichts mehr. Ron erwachte erst aus seiner Starre als er die Wärter lachen hörte. In dem Moment betrat der Polizist, der Ron's Fall leitete, den Raum. Es war David.

«Was ist los, Kumpel?» sagte David zu Ron. «Ich rate dir, das Buch zu öffnen und ein Gebet für deine Partner zu lesen, da sie heute nacht ihre erste Nacht in einer Zelle verbringen werden. Ja- ja, wir haben sie erfolgreich verhaftet.»

pulled the rope three times. It was the signal they agreed to. It meant that everything was ready. Ron was very glad and started to pull the rope back. It did not take him long. Soon he pulled into the room a large bundle through the bars.

«Excellent»! he whispered.

He asked his partners in crime to put a loaded gun into the package. Ron planned to use it against the guards. He hoped to make the guards open the door with the help of the gun. Ron started to unwrap the package. But it was wrapped with the paper and Scotch tape in many layers.

«Idiots!» - Ron thought. – «It's not a Christmas present. What were they thinking about?»

He was angry. As there were no scissors or knife in his cell. He had little time. The tape made a loud noise when Ron began to unwrap the package. Ron started to worry that the guards would hear the noise. Trying not to make noise he began to unwrap the tape layer by layer. It took him forty minutes. Cursing the stupidity of his partners in crime, Ron finally reached the paper. He began to unwrap the paper. Finally, under the paper he saw the box.

«Packed up like in the store» - Ron whispered angrily.

But having carefully examined the box, it appeared to Ron that all seemed to be much worse. It was not the box with the gun, it was ... the Bible.

For a minute Ron just sat and looked at the book. He could not understand anything. Ron came to only when he heard the laughter of the guards. At that moment the policeman who led Ron's case entered the room. It was David.

«What's up, buddy?» David said to Ron, «I advise you to open the book and read a prayer for your partners, as they will spend their first night in a cell tonight. Yes - yes, we arrested them successfully.»

Ron's überraschtes Gesicht ließ David lächeln. «Wir haben gehört, dass du plantest zu fliehen», erklärte David –»Wir haben nachgedacht und entschieden, dass die Bibel nützlicher für dich ist. Also, frohes Lesen, Ron!»

David smiled at Ron's surprise.
«We heard you were planning to escape»,
David explained - «then we considered it
and decided that the Bible will be more
useful for you. Well, enjoy reading, Ron!»

4

Ein Japanischer Vertrag

Davids Ehefrau Anna war die Assistentin des Verkaufsdirektors. Ihre Firma würde einen großen Vertrag mit einer japanischen Firma abschließen. Für die letzte Phase der Verhandlungen reisten Anna und ihr Chef nach Japan. Ihr Chef hieß Nick. Es war eine interessante Geschäftsreise; die Verhandlungen liefen großartig. All warteten auf den Vertragsabschluss. Doch auf einmal weigerten sich die Japaner, ihn zu unterzeichnen. Nick und Ann waren sehr überrascht. Die Japaner gaben ihnen keine Erklärung. Sie baten sie nur, andere Vertreter der Firma nach Japan zu senden. Anna und Nick mussten nach Hause reisen.
«Aber was ist denn passiert?» fragte der Generaldirektor bei ihrem Treffen. «Sie waren bereit, den Vertrag zu unterschreiben. Was habt ihr falsch gemacht?»
 «Es war alles perfekt! Wir verstehen nicht, was

Japanese Contract

David's wife Anna worked as an assistant of the sales director. Their firm was going to sign a big contract with a Japanese company. Anna went to Japan with her chief for the last phase of the negotiations. The chief's name was Nick. The business trip was interesting; the negotiations were going great. Everyone was waiting for the finalization of the contract. But suddenly the Japanese refused to sign it. Nick and Anna were very surprised. The Japanese did not explain anything to them. They just asked to send to Japan other representatives from their firm. Anne and Nick had to go home.
«But what happened?» the Director General asked them when they met.» They were ready to sign the contract. What did you do wrong?»

passiert ist!» sagte Nick. «Wie Sie wissen, habe ich Verhandlungen stets perfekt geführt.»
Der Generaldirektor entschied, einen Spezialisten für Japan-Studien einzustellen. Nick und Anna verbrachten viel Zeit damit, ihm die Einzelheiten der Reise zu beschreiben. Er überprüfte jedes Detail und sagte schließlich:
«Ich glaube ich weiß, welchen Fehler ihr gemacht habt. Versuchen wir mal, das zu checken.»
Ein anderer Handlungsbevollmächtigter ging um die Verhandlungen fortzuführen. Der Spezialist für Japan-Studien traf sich mit ihm vor der Abreise und gab ihm einige Anweisungen.
Einige Tage vergingen und der neue Firmenvertreter kam mit dem unterzeichneten Vertrag zurück!
Nick verstand immer noch nicht – was war los? Er beschloss, den Fachmann für japanische Kultur anzurufen.
«Also, welchen Fehler haben wir gemacht? – fragte Nick.
«Sehen Sie, ich fragte Sie, wie Sie sich am Tisch verhalten haben,» erwiderte er. «Und Sie sagten, dass Sie versucht haben, still und ordentlich zu essen, richtig?»
«Natürlich!» – sagte Nick.
«Tatsache ist, dass Sie damit die Japaner beleidigt haben. Wenn ein Gast beim Essen nicht mampft, zeigt ihnen das, dass ihm das Gericht nicht schmeckt! Die Japaner wollten den Vertrag nicht unterschreiben weil Sie sie beleidigt haben!» – erklärte er.
Ordinäres Mampfen kann Sie also manchmal einen großen Vertrag kosten.

«Everything was perfect! We do not understand what has happened!» Nick said. «You know, I always carry on negotiations perfectly».
The Director General decided to hire a specialist in Japan studies. Nick and Anna described the journey to him in detail for a long time. He verified every detail and finally said:
«I think I understand what your mistake was. Let's try to check».
Another officer went to continue the negotiations. A specialist in Japan studies met him and gave him some instructions before leaving.
A few days have passed and a new officer returned with a signed contract!
Nick still did not understand - what was the matter? He decided to call the specialist in Japanese culture.
«So what was our mistake? - Nick asked.
«You see, I asked you how you behaved at the table,» he replied. «And you said that you tried to eat quietly and neatly, didn't you?»
«Of course!» - Nick said.
«The fact is that it was an insult to the Japanese. When a guest does not champ during the meal, he shows that he does not like the food! The Japanese did not want to sign a contract with you because you have insulted them!» - He explained.
So sometimes the common champ can cost a big contract.

5

Liebe auf den Ersten Blick

David liebte seinen Job als Polizist. Der Gedanke, dass er Recht und Ordnung aufrecht hielt, freute ihn. Manchmal brachte ihm seine Arbeit auch interessante Fälle. David erinnerte sich besonders an den Fall mit einem Räuber namens Jim.
Jim verübte einen großen Banküberfall. Der Überfall verlief ziemlich gut. Dann musste er sich beeilen. Die Polizei war noch nicht bei der Bank eingetroffen, aber Jim wusste, sie würde bald kommen. Er rannte zur Bushaltestelle und bestieg den Bus. Er würde die Stadt für immer verlassen. Er musste die Geldtaschen in den Gepäckraum des Busses legen. Aber Jim war nicht verärgert. Denn falls die Polizei den Bus erwischte, würden sie nicht wissen, wer die Taschen in den Gepäckraum gestellt hatte. Der Bus verließ die Stadt und fuhr mit hoher Geschwindigkeit die Autobahn entlang. Jim

Love at First Sight

David loved his job at the police. He was pleased to think that he maintained law and order. Also interesting cases happened at his work sometimes. David particularly remembered the case of one robber whose name was Jim.
Jim committed a huge bank robbery. The robbery went quite well. Then he had to hurry. The police had not arrived at the bank yet but Jim knew that they would come soon. He ran to the bus station and boarded the intercity bus. He was going to leave the city forever. He had to put the bags with the money into the trunk of the bus. But Jim was not upset. After all, if the police caught the bus, they would not know who put the bags into the trunk of the bus. The bus left the city and drove along the highway at a high speed. Jim realized that the police would

merkte, dass die Polizei ihn nicht einholen würde. Er war in guter Stimmung. Im Bus sah Jim ein hübsches Mädchen. Sie war so bezaubernd, dass Jim seine Augen nicht abwenden konnte. Sie sah zu ihm hin und lächelte. Er vergaß einen Moment, dass er Taschen mit Geld bei sich hatte. Es war Liebe auf den ersten Blick. Der Sitz neben dem Mädchen war leer. Er ging zu ihr und setzte sich neben die Schöne.

«Klar wäre mir gern etwas Besseres für eine Verabredung mit dir eingefallen», sagte er zu ihr. «Aber ich muss sofort von hier weg. Also lass mich dich einfach zu einem Spaziergang einladen. Ich habe noch nie so ein traumhaftes Mädchen gesehen!» sagte er.

Das Mädchen sah in aufmerksam an. Jim war ein großer, gutaussehender Mann. Sie mochte ihn auch.

«Naja», sagte sie. «Warum nicht. Mir ist es recht.» Aber sie wollte ihre Telefonnummer nicht einem Fremden geben.

«Es wäre besser, wenn du mir deine Nummer gibst. Hier ist ein Stift. Schreib sie auf die Busfahrkarte», sagte sie. «Ich rufe dich später an. Mein Name ist Margaret.»

Jim musste zustimmen. Er schrieb seine Telefonnummer und seinen Namen auf seine Busfahrkarte und dann verabschiedeten sie sich voneinander. Das Mädchen verließ den Bus in der nächsten Stadt. Jim fuhr zwei weitere Stunden und stieg dann auch aus. Der Fahrer öffnete den Gepäckraum und... Jim konnte es nicht glauben.

Seine Taschen mit dem Geld waren nicht da! Aber wer konnte sie genommen haben? Es sah nicht nach einem Zufall aus. Der Fahrer sagte ihm, dass er die Taschen gegen ein Busticket ausgehändigt hatte. Das Ticket kam von einem Mädchen, das vor zwei Stunden ausgestiegen war. Der Fahrer schlug Jim vor, die Polizei zu rufen. Jim sah ihn nachdenklich an. Natürlich weigerte er sich, die Polizei zu rufen. In dem Moment läutete sein Handy. Er meldete sich.

«Hallo», sagte Jim.

not catch up with him. He was in a good mood. Jim saw a beautiful girl on the bus. She was so charming that Jim could not take his eyes off her. She looked at him and smiled. For a moment he had forgotten that he had bags of money. It was love at first sight. There was an empty seat near the girl. He came up to her and sat down next to this beauty.

«Of course, I would have liked to think up something better for a date with you,» he said to her. «But I have to escape immediately. So let me just invite you for a walk. I have never seen such a wonderful girl!» He said.

The girl looked at him attentively. Jim was a tall, handsome man. She liked him too.

«Well», she said. «Why not. I do not mind». But she did not want to give her phone number to a stranger.

«It would be better if you gave me your number. Here's a pen. Write it on the bus ticket,» she said. «I'll call you later. My name is Margaret».

Jim had to agree. He wrote his phone number and name on his bus ticket and then they said good bye to each other. The girl came out of the bus in the next city. Jim drove for another two hours and then also left. The bus driver opened the trunk and ... Jim could not believe it. His bags with money were not there! But who could have taken his bags? It did not look like an accident. The driver told him that he gave the bags for a bus ticket. The ticket was produced by a girl who got off a couple of hours ago. The driver suggested to Jim that he call the police. Jim looked thoughtfully at the driver. Of course, he refused to call the police. At this moment his phone rang. He answered it.

«Hello», said Jim.

«Jim, this is Margaret», he heard the voice of the beauty from the bus, «Have you got off the bus already?»

«Jim, hier ist Margaret», hörte er die Stimme der Schönen aus dem Bus, «hast du den Bus schon verlassen?»
Jim schwieg eine Weile. Dann antwortete er.
«Wie wusstest du von dem Geld, Margaret?» fragte er nervös.
«Tut mir leid, ich konnte der Versuchung nicht widerstehen», sagte sie, «ich hörte im Radio von dem Überfall. Die Beschreibung des Räubers passte zu deinem Aussehen. Deine weit offenen Augen und deine nervöse Miene sagten mir, dass du der von der Polizei Gesuchte bist», sagte sie, «du bist ohne Taschen in den Bus gestiegen und mir war klar, sie mussten im Gepäckraum sein. Und du hast mir deine Busfahrkarte gegeben, erinnerst du dich?»
«Ich habe das Geld aus der Bank geholt und es gehört mir!» rief Jim und ging vom Bus weg, «gib mir zumindest die Hälfte zurück!»
«Deine aufgeregte Stimme ist nicht so überzeugend wie mein Lächeln. Ich werde dir das Geld nicht geben, Jim. Du bist ein Mann, du kannst eine andere Bank überfallen. Aber sei vorsichtig bei fremden Frauen. Verzeih mir und mach's gut!»
«Ich werde dich finden, Margaret! Und dann wird es dir leid tun, mich getäuscht zu haben!» rief Jim, doch Margaret hatte aufgelegt.
Ein paar Tage später rief Margaret ihn wieder an. Sie sagte, ihr Gewissen plagte sie und sie wollte ihm die Hälfte des Geldes zurückgeben. Außerdem mochte sie, Jim hoffte, ihn besser kennen zu lernen.
Sie machte ein Treffen mit ihm aus und Jim kam zur vereinbarten Zeit an den vereinbarten Ort. Doch statt Margaret und die Geldtaschen warteten mehrere Polizisten auf ihn.
Auf der Polizeistation fragte Jim ob Margaret verhaftet wurde. David sagte Jim, dass ein Mädchen bei der Polizei angerufen hatte. Sie sagte, sie wüsste wie der Räuber gefasst werden könnte. Sie hatte sich mit Jim verabredet, doch plötzlich sah sie ein Foto von ihm in den Nachrichten. Sie war sehr

Jim was silent for a while. Then he answered.
«How did you get to know about the money, Margaret?» He asked nervously.
«Sorry, I could not resist the temptation,» she said, «I heard on the radio about the robbery. The description of the robber coincided with your appearance. Your wide open eyes and the nervous expression on your face told me that you were the one the police were looking for,» she said, «You got on the bus without bags and I realized that they were in the trunk of the bus. And you gave me your bus ticket yourself. Do you remember?»
«I took the money from the bank and it's mine!» Jim cried, moving away from the bus, «Give me back at least half!»
«Your nervous cry is not as convincing as my smile. I will not give you the money, Jim. You're a man so you can rob another bank. But be careful with strange women. Forgive me and good bye!»
«I will find you, Margaret! And then you'll be sorry for deceiving me!» Jim cried, but Margaret had hung up.
A few days have passed and Margaret called him again. She said that she was conscience-stricken and she wanted to give him back half the money. Besides, she liked Jim very much and she hoped to get to know him better. She set a meeting with him and Jim came at the appointed time to the appointed place. But a several policemen waited for him instead of Margaret and the bags with money.
At the police station Jim asked David if Margaret was arrested. David told Jim that a girl called the police. She said she knew how to find the robber. She set a date with Jim but suddenly she saw his picture in the news. She was very upset that he was a robber ... And she had no choice but to call the police and tell them when and where the robber would come. But when Jim told his

aufgebracht weil er ein Räuber war ... Und sie hatte keine Wahl außer die Polizei zu informieren und ihnen zu sagen, wann und wohin der Räuber kommen würde.
Aber als Jim seine Geschichte erzählte, sah David ihn lange nachdenklich an. «Einer Frau bedrohen ist ein sehr großes Risiko», sagte er schließlich zu Jim, «Frauen verzeihen Drohungen nicht.»
«Ja. Eine Frau bedrohen ist gefährlicher als eine Bank zu überfallen,» sagte Jim nervös.

story David thoughtfully stared at him for a long time.
«Threatening a woman is a very big risk,» he finally said to Jim, «Women do not forgive threats.»
«Yes. To threaten a woman is more dangerous than to rob a bank,» Jim said nervously.

6

Fußball

Davids Vater Christian wurde am Sonntag 50 Jahre alt. Seine Frau Linda war morgens schon sehr aufgeregt. Sie wollte, dass die Feier gut wurde, da sie alle ihre Verwandten und viele Freunde dazu eingeladen hatten. Am Abend war das Haus voller Gäste.
Christian empfing sie in einem weißen Anzug mit einer Fliege.
«Christian, du siehst toll aus!» – sagte eine seiner Nichten. «Du siehst nicht aus wie ein Fünfzigjähriger sondern wie dreißig!» «Jetzt aber! Du übertreibst» – sagte Christian, obwohl er sich wirklich darüber freute.
Christian erhielt viele verschiedene Geschenke. Die Party war toll. Alle feierten und hatten Spass. Doch die Gastgeber nicht gedacht. Auf der Feier waren viele Kinder, doch die Erwachsenen beachteten die Kids nicht. Alle Gäste holten sich etwas zu essen, sie stießen auf Christian an und gratulierten ihm. Keiner kümmerte sich um die Kinder, die unter sich spielten. Zuerst war ihnen etwas langweilig. Dann beschlossen sie, Fußball zu spielen.
«Gib uns einen Ball!» bat ein Kind Anna.
«David, wo finden wir einen Ball für die

Football

David's father Christian turns 50 years old this Sunday. His wife Linda has been very nervous since the very morning. She wanted the party to go well, as they invited all their relatives and many friends to the anniversary. In the evening their house was full of guests.
Christian met them dressed in a beautiful white costume with a bow tie.
«Christian, you look awesome!»- one of his nieces said. «You look not like a man of fifty but of thirty!»
«Come on! You're exaggerating» - Christian said, although he was very pleased indeed. Christian was presented with many different gifts. The party was going great. Everybody was celebrating and having fun. But the hosts hadn't thought of one thing. There were many children at the celebration, but adults didn't pay attention to the kids. All the guests helped themselves to food, they made toasts, and congratulated Christian. Nobody took care of the children and they played on their own. At first they were bored a little. Then they decided to

19

Kinder?» fragte sie ihren Mann.
«Ich werde einen suchen!» versprach David. Aber in dem Moment wurde er von einem Gast gerufen und vergaß den Ball sofort. Plötzlich bemerkte eines der Kinder, dass eine große Flasche Cola vom Tisch gefallen war.
«Oh, nehmen wir doch die anstatt des Balles!» schlug einer der Jungen vor. Den Kindern gefiel die Idee. Sie nahmen die Flasche und gingen in den Hof. Dort teilten sie sich in Teams auf und fingen an, mit der Colaflasche Fußball zu spielen. Sie machten die Tore aus Steinen.
Es stellte sich heraus, dass die Flasche einen super Fußball abgab. Sie spielten etwa fünf Minuten lang. Dann waren sie es leid und gingen zu den Gästen ins Haus zurück.
Die Erwachsenen waren in Hochstimmung. Sie waren gerade für ein großes Gruppenfoto aufgestanden. David übernahm die Rolle des Fotografen.
«Rückt näher zusammen! Ihr seid eine richtig große Schar!» rief er den Gästen zu.
«Ich habe es immer gehasst, auf Geburtstagen fotografiert zu werden!» grummelte Christian, «diese Fotos sind immer so langweilig und sehen alle gleich aus.» Dann kam eines der Kinder zu Christian und meinte:
«Großvater, ich habe Durst!» Christian nahm die Flasche vom Tisch und öffnete sie. Und dann kam ein Cola-Springbrunnen auf alle herab. Es war die Colaflasche, mit der Kinder Fußball gespielt hatten.
Christians weißer Anzug und die schönen Kleider der Frauen – alles war jetzt mit Cola bedeckt! So etwas hatte natürlich keiner erwartet. David fasst sich als erster.
«Oh, toll!» sagte er. «Christian, alles ist so wie du es dir gewünscht hast! Dieses Mal werden die Fotos ungewöhnlich und nicht so langweilig sein!»

play football.
«Give us a ball!» A child asked Anna.
«David, where can we find a ball for the children?» She asked her husband.
«I'll look for it!» David promised.
But at that moment one of the guests called him and he immediately forgot about the ball. Suddenly one of the children noticed that a big bottle of Coke fell off the table.
«Oh, let's use it instead of the ball!» One of the boys offered. The kids liked the idea. They took the bottle and went into the yard. There they divided into teams and started to play football with a bottle of Coke. They made the gates from stones. It turned out that the bottle was a great ball for playing football. They played for about five minutes. Then they got tired and returned to the house to all the guests. The adults were in high spirits. They had just gotten up to take a big group photo. David played the role of the photographer.
«Get closer to each other! You're a real crowd!» He shouted to the guests.
«I've always hated to be photographed at birthdays!» Christian grumbled, «These photos always turn out to be so boring and all alike.»
Then one of the kids came up to Christian and asked:
«Grandfather, I'm thirsty!» He said. Christian took the bottle from the table and opened it. And then a fountain Coke came down on everyone. It was the bottle of Coke that the children had been playing football with. Christian's white costume and women's beautiful dresses - everything was now covered with Coke! Of course, no one expected this. David was the first who came around.
«Oh, great!» He said. «Christian, everything happens as you'd wished! This time the photos will be unusual and not so boring!»

7

Eine Verfolgungsjagd

David hatte Dienst und erhielt einen Anruf. Zwei verdächtige Männer standen in der Nähe des Autos, das im Hof eines der Häuser geparkt war. Die Nachbarn bemerkten sie und riefen die Polizei. David und sein Partner erschienen schnell am Ort des Vorfalls.
Die Nacht war dunkel und die Straße war verlassen und schlecht beleuchtet, doch die Polizei fand die Autodiebe schnell. Doch die Diebe bemerkten die Polizisten ebenfalls schnell. Natürlich warteten die Diebe nicht bis die Handschellen klickten.
Sie verließen das Auto sofort und begannen um ihr Leben zu rennen. Selbstverständlich fingen die Polizisten sofort an, sie zu verfolgen und die Jagd begann. Die Verbrecher verschwanden in den engen Gassen zwischen den Häusern.
Das Auto konnte dort nicht fahren und David und sein Partner fingen an zu laufen und sie zu Fuß zu verfolgen. Die Verfolgung machte viel Lärm und sorgte dafür, dass die Hunde in der Nachbarschaft zu bellen anfingen.
Lautes Bellen übertönte den Klang von Schritten. Und nach einer Biegung begriffen

A Pursuit

Once when David was on duty he received a call. Two suspicious men stood near the car parked in the yard of one of the houses. The neighbors saw them and called the police. David and his partner quickly reported to the scene of the incident.
The night was dark and the street was deserted and poorly lit, but the police quickly found the car thieves. Yet the thieves noticed the Police immediately too. Naturally, the guys did not wait until the handcuffs were put on them. They left the car immediately and ran for life from the police. Of course, the police began to follow them and the pursuit began. Criminals turned to the narrow passages between the houses. The car could not drive there and David and his partner started to run and pursue them. The pursuit produced a lot of noise, and because of that all the dogs in the neighborhood started barking. Loud barking drowned out the sound of footsteps. And after one of the turns the police suddenly understood that they had lost the criminals!

die Polizisten auf einmal, dass sie die Verbrecher verloren hatten!
«Was machen wir jetzt?» sagte einer der Polizisten verärgert. «Sie waren direkt vor uns! Sie könnten weit kommen!»
David schaute auf den hohen Zaun. Plötzlich sprang einer Verbrecher über den Zaun und der zweite folgte.
«Wir ergeben uns!» sagte der eine.
Beide hatten Angst. Nach dem Überraschungsmoment nahmen die Polizisten ihr Angebot gern an.
«Es ist gut, dass ihr entschieden habt, euch der Polizei zu ergeben», bemerkte David während er ihnen Handschellen anlegte. «Aber eben noch sah euer Plan ganz anders aus. Wieso die Änderung?» fragte er.
«Da waren zwei riesige Hunde!» sagte einer der Verbrecher. «Als ich sie sah, realisierte ich, dass der Richter sicherlich netter zu mir wird als diese beiden Hunde!»
«Ihr solltet nicht über einen Zaun springen wenn ihr nicht wisst, was dahinter ist» sagte David.

«What are we going to do?» one of the policemen said angrily. «They were right in front of us! They could have gotten far!»
David looked at the high fence. Suddenly one of the criminals jumped over the fence and then the second one did the same.
«We surrender!» One of them said.
They were both scared. After a moment of surprise the policemen gladly accepted their offer.
«It is good that you decided to surrender to the police» David noted while putting handcuffs on them. «But only a moment ago your plan was quite different. Why did it change?» He asked.
«There were two huge dogs!» One of the criminals said. «When I saw them I realized that the judge will definitely be kinder to me than those two dogs!»
«You should not jump over the fence if you don't know what's behind it» said David.

Ein Schlechtes Horoskop

Roberts Schwester Gaby hatte eine ältere Schwiegermutter, die bei Gaby und ihrem Mann lebte. Diese Oma hatte zwei Leidenschaften. Sie glaubte fest an Horoskope und sie liebte ihr altes Sofa. Sie hatte das Sofa vor fünfzig Jahren zur ihrer Hochzeit bekommen. Oma war damals 16. Und jetzt knarrte das Sofa ganz schrecklich und war ständig kaputt. Klar, keiner mochte es. Und dann entschlossen sich Gaby und ihr Mann, in ein neues Haus zu ziehen. Gaby wollte das hässliche alte Sofa nicht mitnehmen.
«Man kann nicht mal darauf sitzen!» versuchte Gaby ihre Schwiegermutter zu überreden. «Wir kaufen dir statt dessen ein tolles neues Sofa!»
Aber Oma weigerte sich beharrlich, es wegzuwerfen.
«Nein! Niemals! Ich werde am Montag den Handwerker anrufen», sagte die Oma resolut, «und das Sofa wird wieder wie neu sein.

A Bad Horoscope

Robert's sister Gaby had an elderly mother in law. She lived with Gaby and her husband. And this grandmother had two passions. She totally believed in horoscopes and loved her old sofa. She was given this sofa as a gift fifty years ago on her wedding. The granny was 16 years old then. And now this old sofa creaked badly and broke down all the time. Of course, nobody liked it. And then Gaby and her husband decided to move to a new house. Gaby did not want to carry there this ugly old sofa.
«One can not even sit on it!» Gaby tried to persuade her mother in law. «Let's buy you a great new sofa instead!»
But the granny absolutely refused to throw it away.
«No! Never! I'll call the repairman this Monday,» the granny said resolutely, «and the sofa will be as good as new. People could do things of such high quality back then! And it was written in today's horoscope that I

Damals machten die Leute noch hochwertige Dinge! Und mein Horoskop von heute sagt, ich soll nichts wegwerfen.»

Dann kam Gaby eine Idee. Sie beschloss, eine Leidenschaft ihrer Schwiegermutter mit der anderen zu bekämpfen. Gaby hatte einen Freund, der bei der Zeitung arbeitete. Ihre Oma kaufte die Zeitung mit dem Horoskop darin. Gaby überredete ihren Freund, das Montags-Horoskop ihrer Oma zu ändern.

«In Ordnung! Was soll ich dann schreiben?» fragte er Gaby. Gaby hatte sich schon einen Text ausgedacht.

«Ihr Plan für den heutigen Tag wird scheitern. Vergessen Sie Ihr Vorhaben für heute! Es ist besser, jemanden zu beschenken. Werfen Sie unnötige Dinge weg,» diktierte Gaby. Ihr Freund schrieb alles auf und versprach, den Text zu veröffentlichen.

Es wurde Montag. Oma las wie üblich ihr Horoskop in der Zeitung. Und es verwirrte sie etwas. Gaby bemerkte es als sie sich für die Arbeit fertig machte. Sie hoffte sehr, dass es funktionierte. Am Abend kamen Gaby und ihr Mann voller Hoffnung nach Hause. Es wäre toll, wenn das alte, kaputte Sofa endlich verschwände! Sie kamen nach Hause und sahen das alte Sofa und eine sehr geknickte Oma.

«Was ist passiert? Warum bist du so traurig?» fragte Gabys Ehemann die Oma.

«Seht, ich habe heute morgen einen Lottoschein gekauft», sagte sie. «Aber dann habe ich das heutige Horoskop gelesen. Es sagt, heute ist kein Glückstag und so gab ich den Lottoschein unserer Nachbarin. Und stellt euch vor – sie hat gerade Fünfzigtausend gewonnen!» sagte Oma. Gaby und ihr Mann sahen sich überrascht und frustriert an. Wir hatten so ein Pech mit diesem Horoskop!

«Ärgert euch nicht so», sagte Oma zu ihnen. «Ich habe schon ein anderes Los gekauft. Und übrigens hat der Handwerker mein Sofa repariert. Jetzt bin ich für den Umzug bereit.»

should not throw away anything».

Then an idea occurred to Gaby. She decided to combat one of her mother-in-law's passions with another. Gaby had a friend who worked in the newspaper. Her granny bought that newspaper with the horoscopes. Gaby persuaded her friend to change her granny's horoscope for Monday.

«All right! So what should we write then?» He asked Gaby. Gaby has already thought out a text.

«Today's plan will fail. Forget about your today's intentions! It is better to make a gift to anyone. Throw away unnecessary things,» Gaby dictated.

Her friend wrote everything down and promised to publish the text.

Monday came. Granny read her horoscope in the newspaper as usual. And it puzzled her a little bit. Gaby noticed it when she was preparing to go for work. She hoped very much that this would work.

In the evening Gaby and her husband came home feeling hopeful. It would be great if the old broken sofa finally disappeared! They came home and saw the old sofa and a very upset granny.

«What happened? Why are you so sad?» Gaby's husband asked the granny.

«You see, this morning I bought a lottery ticket,» she said. «But then I read the horoscope for today. It said that it was an unfortunate day, and I gave the lottery ticket to our neighbor. And just think of it - she just won fifty thousand!» The granny said.

Gaby and her husband looked at each other with surprise and frustration. We were so unlucky with this horoscope!

«Do not worry so much,» the granny told them. «I already bought another ticket. And by the way the repairman fixed my sofa. Now I'm ready to move.»

9

Ein Sehr Dringender Anruf

Robert und David untersuchten einen Raubüberfall. Der Hausbesitzer, ein älterer Mann, erzählte ihnen, was passiert war. Ein Mann klopfte an die Tür und bat den Besitzer um Erlaubnis, telefonieren zu dürfen. Er sagte, er müsse ein sehr dringendes Ortsgespräch führen und die Batterie seines Handy war leer. Der Besitzer war gutgelaunt und ließ ihn ins Haus. Der ungebetene Gast betrat das Zimmer und griff nach dem Telefon. Er sah sich um und überzeugte sich, dass sonst niemand im Haus war. Er entschied, dass der ältliche Besitzer harmlos war.
«Bringen Sie alles Wertvolle hierher,» sagte er zu ihm. Aber der Besitzer war kein Feigling. Der schwarze Gewehrlauf war bereits auf den Räuber gerichtet!
«Verschwinden Sie jetzt aus meinem Haus!» sagte der Besitzer. Der Räuber musste sehr

A Very Urgent Call

Once Robert and David came to investigate a robbery case. The elderly owner of the house told them what had happened. Some man knocked on the door and asked the owner for permission to call. He said that he needed to make a very urgent call to a local number and his mobile phone had a very low battery. The owner was in a good humor and let him into the house. The uninvited guest entered the room and grabbed the phone. He looked around and made sure that there was no one else in the house. He decided that the old owner was harmless.
«Bring here everything valuable,» he told him.
But the owner was not a coward. The black barrel of a gun was already pointed at the robber!

schnell abhauen. Die Polizei kam nach zehn Minuten, da war er natürlich schon fort.
«Haben Sie die Polizei mit dem Telefon angerufen, das vom Räuber benutzt wurde?» – fragte David den Besitzer. «Ja, habe ich,» bestätigte dieser.
«Also sind wahrscheinlich keine Fingerabdrücke mehr vorhanden», vermutete David. «Naja, wir werden versuchen, ihn zu finden. Beschreiben Sie ihn noch mal in allen Einzelheiten und wir nehmen alles in den Bericht auf.»
Plötzlich läutete das Telefon. Der Besitzer wechselte Blicke mit den Polizisten und meldete sich. Der Anrufer war eine fremde junge Frau. «Guten Morgen,» sagte sie höflich. «Können Sie Charlie ans Telefon holen? Er hat mich vor kurzem von dieser Nummer aus angerufen.»
«Charlie hat sie vor kurzem von dieser Nummer angerufen?» meinte er abwesend. Der Hausbesitzer hatte heute nur die Polizei angerufen… Das hieß, der Räuber hatte diese Frau angerufen! Robert verstand sofort, was das bedeutete! Er schrieb schnell die Nummer auf und in ein paar Minuten hatten sie die Adresse der Frau ausfindig gemacht und fuhren hin.
Roberts Vermutung hatte sich bestätigt. Der Räuber war dort! Es stellte sich heraus, dass er nach dem Betreten des Hauses keine bessere Idee hatte als seine Ehefrau anzurufen! Und dieser Fehler kostete ihn seine Freiheit. Natürlich nahmen David und sein Team den unglücklichen Räuber sofort fest.

«Get out of my house now!» the owner said. The robber had to leave very quickly. The police came in just ten minutes but, of course, he was already gone.
«Did you call the police from the phone which was used by the robber?» - David asked the owner.
«Yes, I did,» he confirmed.
«So the fingerprints are probably gone,» David assumed. «Well, we'll try to find him. Describe him in details again, and we'll write everything into the report.»
Suddenly the telephone rang. The owner exchanged glances with the police and picked it up. It was an unknown young woman.
«Good morning,» she said politely. «Can you call Charlie to the phone? He called me from this number recently.»
«Did Charlie call you recently from this number?» He asked absently.
Today the owner of the house called only the police ... It means that the robber called this woman! Robert immediately understood what it all meant! He quickly wrote down the number and in a few minute they determined the woman's address and went there. Robert's guess was confirmed. The robber was there! It turns out that having entered the house he could not invent something better than to call his own wife! And this mistake cost him his freedom. Of course, David and his team immediately arrested the unfortunate robber.

10

Die Gäste

David freundete sich vor kurzem mit einem seiner Kollegen an. Der Name des Kollegen war Tom. Tom war ein Vorgesetzter, aber er und David hatten viele gemeinsame Interessen. David lud Tom zu sich nach Hause ein. Davids Ehefrau Anna kaufte einen leckeren Schokokuchen. Zur vereinbarten Zeit läutete es an der Tür. Es war Tom. David öffnete und bat ihn herein. Ein großer struppiger Hund kam mit Tom ins Haus. David streichelte seinen Kopf und der Hund kam ins Zimmer. David, Anna und Tom setzen sich ins Wohnzimmer und der Hund wanderte durch die anderen Zimmer. Sie unterhielten sich über die Arbeit. Anfangs unterhielten sie sich über Probleme auf der Arbeit. Dann begannen sie, über Urlaubspläne zu reden. Der Abend verlief großartig.
«Übrigens, der Chef unserer Abteilung liebt Football», sagte Tom. «Letztes Wochenende haben wir zusammen gespielt.»

The Guests

Recently David became friends with one of his colleague. The colleague's name was Tom. Tom was a senior officer, but he had a lot of common interests with David. Once David invited Tom to his place. David's wife Anne bought a delicious chocolate cake. And at the appointed time the doorbell rang. It was Tom. David opened the door and invited him in. A huge shaggy dog entered the house with Tom.
David petted his head and the dog entered the room. David, Anne and Tom sat down in the living room and the dog went for a walk through other rooms. They talked about work. At the beginning they talked about problems at work. Then they started talking about plans for the holiday. The evening was going great.
«By the way, the head of our department loves football,» Tom said. «Last weekend we played football together.»
 «Really? I did not know,» David said.

«Echt? Das wusste ich nicht,» sagte David. «Vielleicht möchtest du mit uns spielen?» schlug Tom vor. «Ja, das wäre toll. Ich habe lange nicht Football gespielt. Aber in der High School war ich ein Football-Spieler,» sagte David.
Plötzlich kam aus der Küche ein fürchterlicher Krach.
«Ich werde mal nachsehen, was da los ist,» sagte David.
Er kam in die Küche und sah die schreckliche Szene. Der Vorhang war abgerissen und das hatte soviel Lärm gemacht. Der riesige struppige Hund zerlegte gerade einen Stuhl! Und es sollte erwähnt werden, dass er das ganz toll machte. Die Reste des Schokokuchens lagen auf dem Boden. Der Hund mochte den Kuchen vermutlich, denn er hatte ihn ganz aufgefressen!
David war geschockt von der Szene, die sich ihm bot. Nach ein paar Minuten fasste er sich. In dem Moment wusste er nicht, was er tun sollte, da Tom ihn gerade eingeladen hatte, mit dem Chef ihrer Abteilung Football zu spielen. David war noch nicht so lange bei der Polizei und er wollte natürlich zur Polizeifamilie gehören. Ja, und er wollte auch eine nützliche Bekanntschaft machen. Warum sollte er sich also über das Benehmen des Hundes beschweren? David beschloss, es war nicht der richtige Zeitpunkt dafür. Er ging wieder ins Wohnzimmer.
«Was ist da passiert?» fragte Tom.
«Es ist alles in Ordnung,» erwiderte David. «Mach dir nichts draus.» Ein leises Rascheln ertönte aus der Küche. David begriff, der Hund zerfetzte weiter die Stühle…
Endlich war Tom soweit, nach Hause zu gehen. Der Hund rannte durchs Haus während er sich im Flur die Jacke anzog. Am Ende zerbrach der die Blumentöpfe im Wohnzimmer und machte ein Pfütze auf den Teppich. Tom sah es sich ruhig an und sagte nichts. David wollte, dass die Gäste früher gingen. Schnell verabschiedete er sich von

«Maybe you want to play with us?» Tom suggested.
«Yes, it would be great. I have not played football for a long time. Though I took part in football matches at high school,» David said.
Suddenly a terrible noise was heard from the kitchen.
«I'll go there and look what is the matter,» David said.
He came into the kitchen and saw a terrible scene there. The curtain was torn off. It was the curtain what produced so much noise. The huge shaggy dog was tearing a chair at this very moment! And it should be mentioned that the dog was doing a great job. The remains of the chocolate cake were on the floor. The dog probably liked the cake because it ate all of it!
David was stunned by the scene he saw. In a few minutes he came to. At that moment he did not know what to do, since Tom had just invited him to play football with the head of their department. David worked in the police not so long time, and, of course, he wanted to become part of the police family. Yes, and he also wanted to make a useful acquaintance. Why should he complain of the behavior of the dog then? David decided that it was the wrong time to do so. He returned to the living room.
«What happened there?» Tom asked.
«Everything is fine,» David replied. «Never mind.»
A quiet rustling could be heard from the kitchen. David understood that the dog continued to tear the chairs …
Finally, Tom was ready to go home. The dog was running around the house while he was dressing in the hallway. In the end it broke the flower pots in the living room and made a pool on the carpet. Tom looked at it calmly and said nothing. David wanted the guests to leave sooner. He quickly said goodbye to Tom. Suddenly he saw that Tom did not call the dog with him.

Tom. Plötzlich sah er, dass Tom den Hund nicht zu sich rief.
«Vergiss deinen Hund nicht,» sagte David.
Tom schaute ihn erstaunt an.
«Ich dachte, das ist dein Hund,» sagte er.

«Do not forget to take your dog,» David said.
Tom looked at him in a surprise.
«I thought it was your dog,» he said.

11

Ein Unglücklicher Raubüberfall

Larry bereitete einen Überfall auf einen Laden vor. Er wählte den passenden Zeitpunkt – direkt vor dem Schließen. Zu der Zeit waren keine Kunden im Laden und die Tageseinnahmen waren noch in der Kasse. Larry folgerte, dass die junge Verkäuferin sofort Angst bekommen und ihm alles Geld geben würde.
Und natürlich hatte sie keinen Grund, dummen Heldenmut zu zeigen. Sie hatte sich kürzlich mit einen neuen Verehrer getroffen. Und die Einnahmen des Ladens waren immer gut.
In den letzten Tagen hatte er den Laden oft beobachtet. Er dachte nur an den Raubüberfall. Er ging in Gedanken gern alle Details durch. Er dachte, dass er alles perfekt geplant hatte.
Am von ihm bestimmten Tag betrat Larry das Geschäft. Er ging zur Verkäuferin und

An Unfortunate Robbery

Larry prepared to rob a store. He chose an appropriate time - the time right before the closing. At that time there were no visitors at the shop and the daily revenue was still in the cash register. Larry figured that a young saleswoman would be scared at once and would give him all the money. And, of course, she had no reason to demonstrate stupid heroism. Recently she met a new suitor. And the revenue in the store is always good. During the last few days he often surveilled the shop. He did not think about anything except the robbery. He liked to think over all the details. He thought that he planned everything perfectly.
On the appointed day Larry entered the store. He came up to the saleswoman and greeted her politely. She smiled at him and asked how she could help him. He asked her to show him a small vacuum cleaner. The

begrüßte sie höflich. Sie lächelte ihn an und fragte, wie sie ihm helfen könne. Er bat sie, ihm einen kleinen Staubsauger zu zeigen. Die Verkäuferin nahm den Staubsauger und begann, Larry die Vorzüge zu beschreiben. Larry sah sich im Raum um und ging näher zur Verkäuferin. Engagiert erklärte sie ihm den Staubsauger. Alles lief so wie er es sich vorgestellt hatte! Es war wunderbar.
«Hände hoch, das ist ein Überfall!» Larry rief den Satz, den er lange vorher geübt hatte und zeigte der Verkäuferin sein Messer. «Legen Sie das Geld in die Tasche, schnell!» befahl er ihr.
Überrascht ließ sie den Staubsauger fallen, direkt auf Larrys Fuß und Larry setzte sich stöhnend auf den Boden.
Natürlich rannte die Verkäuferin sofort aus dem Laden und rief um Hilfe. Larry erhob sich ächzend und ging mit Mühe zu einem anderen Ladenausgang. Als die Polizei eintraf und zwei Beamte den Laden betraten, war Larry fort.
David war einer der Polizisten. Er schlug seinem Partner vor, hinaus zu gehen und den Parkplatz abzusuchen. Sie gingen hinaus, checkten das Gebiet um den Laden, doch es war niemand zu sehen. Die Polizisten kamen zur ihrem Auto.
In dem Moment ging der elektronische Alarm los. Die Polizisten blieben stehen und sahen sich an. Sie hatten den Alarm nicht ausgelöst. Sie gingen dem Ton nach und kamen zu den Bäumen nahe des Parkplatzes. David sah sich um, doch da war niemand.
«Also, ist es Zeit aufzuwachen?» fragte Davids Kollege und sah nach oben. David schaute hoch und sah Larry auf einem Ast sitzen.
«Nein. Es ist Zeit, die Fische zu füttern,» erwiderte Larry, «ich habe ein Aquarium zuhause,» fügte er lächelnd hinzu. Die Polizisten waren erheitert.
«Komm herunter. Deine Fische werden lange warten müssen,» David lächelte zurück.

saleswoman took a vacuum cleaner and began to describe its qualities to Larry. Larry looked around the room and came closer to the saleswoman. She heartily described him the vacuum cleaner. Everything was going exactly as he had imagined! It was wonderful.
«Hands up, this is a robbery!» Larry shouted the phrase which he prepared long before and showed a knife to the saleswoman.
«Put the money into the bag quickly!» He commanded to her. She dropped the vacuum cleaner in surprise. It fell on Larry's foot and he sat down on the floor with a groan.
Of course, the saleswoman immediately ran out of the store and began calling for help. Larry got up with a groan and walked with difficulty to another exit from the store. When the police arrived and two police officers entered the store Larry was gone. David was one of the policemen. He suggested to his partner that they go out and search the parking lot. They went out and examined the area around the store, but nobody was there. The policemen came up to their car. At that moment an electronic alarm rang out. The policemen stopped and looked at each other. The signal was not produced by them. They went toward the sound and came up to the trees near the parking lot. David looked around, but nobody was there.
«Well, is it time to wake up?» David's colleague asked looking upwards. David looked up and saw Larry sitting on a tree branch.
«No. It's time to feed the fish,» Larry replied, «I have an aquarium with fish at home,» he added with a smile. The policemen cheered up.
«Come down. Your fish will wait for you for a long time now,» David smiled back.
The robber jumped down to the ground with a groan and the policemen saw that he had a foot injury. They handcuffed him and helped him to get to the police car.

Der Räuber sprang mit einem Ächzen zu Boden und die Beamten sahen, dass sein Fuß verletzt war. Sie legten ihm Handschellen an und halfen ihm zum Polizeiwagen.
«Gut gemacht!» sagte David zu seinem Partner. «Ich wette, dass alle Zeitungen über diesen Raubüberfall schreiben werden. So ein Unsinn passiert nicht jeden Tag!»
«Ja, genau!» stimmte der andere Polizist zu. «Der Kerl beschloss, einen Laden auszurauben und es fällt ihm ein Staubsauger auf den Fuß – das ist doch vollkommener Nonsens!»

«Well done!» David said to his partner. «I bet that all the newspapers will write about this robbery. Such nonsense does not happen every day!»
«Yeah, of course!» another police officer agreed. «The guy decided to rob a store and got a vacuum cleaner dropped on his foot - that's just perfect nonsense!»

12

Ein Ausgestopftes Tier

In der Nähe von Lena und Roberts Haus war ein netter Park. Er war sehr schön und Lena ging gern dort spazieren. Manchmal sogar morgens vor der Arbeit. Einmal fand sie im Winter ein erfrorenes Eichhörnchen. Lena beschloss, es einem Freund zu geben. Dieser machte ausgestopfte Tiere für ein Museum. Lena wollte, dass er ein ausgestopftes Eichhörnchen machte. Sie brachte das Eichhörnchen nach Hause und legte es eine Kuchenschachtel. Dann machte sie sich schnell für die Arbeit fertig.
Ein paar Stunden später rief Robert Lena an. Er war geschäftlich unterwegs und kam erst nachmittags nach Hause.
«Wie fühlst du dich?» fragte er Lena am Telefon. «Super. Was gibt es denn?» erwiderte Lena. «Warum fragst du?»
«Ich denke, du arbeitest zuviel in letzter Zeit,» antwortete Robert. «Ich dachte, du brauchst etwas Erholung.»
«Es geht mir gut, mein Lieber,» wiederholte

A Stuffed Animal

There was a lovely park near Lena and Robert's house. It was very beautiful and Lena loved to walk there. Sometimes she even went there for a walk before work in the morning. Once in winter she found there a frozen squirrel. Lena decided to give it to a friend. He made stuffed animals for a museum. Lena wanted him to make a stuffed squirrel. She took the squirrel home and put it into a box from a cake. Then she prepared herself quickly and left for work.
A few hours later Robert called Lena. He was on a business trip and came back home only in the afternoon.
«How are you feeling?» he asked Lena by phone.
«Excellent. And what is the matter?» Lena answered. «Why did you ask that?»
«I guess you worked too much lately,» Robert replied. «I thought that you need some rest.»
«I'm all right, dear», Lena repeated.

Lena.
«Warst du gestern vielleicht auf der Party?» fragte Robert.
«Nein, ich war zuhause. Das sagte ich dir doch,» meinte Lena. «Warum stellst du so seltsame Fragen?»
«Trotzdem gehst du besser nach Hause, jetzt sofort», Robert bestand darauf. «Es schien mir, dass dir ist etwas Schlimmes passiert.»
«Ich sagte dir, alles ist wunderbar» – erklärte Lena. Sie fing an, die ... zu verlieren.
Doch Robert blieb hartnäckig. Er dachte, sie sollte sofort nach Hause kommen. Anfangs war Lena ärgerlich. Doch dann merkte sie, Robert klang merkwürdig. Lena begann, sich Sorgen zu machen und entschloss sich, früher nach Hause zu gehen.
Sobald sie den Flur betrat, erkannte sie warum Robert so besorgt war. Als ein Eichhörnchen durch die Tür gesprungen kam, wusste Lena was passiert war.
Es stellte sich heraus, dass das Eichhörnchen lebte. Es war nur sehr kalt. Aber als Lena es ins Haus brachte, wurde es in der Wärme wieder lebendig. Es fand einen Stapel Pfannkuchen auf dem Tisch, die Lena für Robert gebacken hatte. Das Eichhörnchen hängte alle Pfannkuchen zum Trocknen überall im Haus auf. Genauso wie es draußen Pilze auf Baumzweige legte. Jetzt hingen die Pfannkuchen überall: vom Sofa, auf dem Regal im Flur, auf den Stühlen ... Als Robert nach Hause kam, bekam das Eichhörnchen Angst und versteckte sich. Robert sah, dass alles im Haus mit Pfannkuchen bedeckt war ... Und auf dem Tisch war eine Nachricht von Lena: «Süßer, die sind für dich.»

«Maybe you were at the party yesterday?» Robert asked.
«No, I was at home. I told you,» Lena said. «Why do you ask such strange questions?»
«Still you better come home right now», Robert insisted. «It seemed to me that something bad happened to you.»
«I told you that everything is fine» - Lena explained. She began to lose her temper. But Robert kept on insisting. He thought that she had to come home right at that time. Lena got angry at first. But then she realized that Robert had a very strange voice. Lena began to worry and decided to go home earlier.
As soon as she entered the hall she realized why Robert was so worried. When a squirrel jumped out of the door Lena realized what had happened.
It turned out that the squirrel was alive. It was just very cold. But when Lena brought it into the house, it came to life with the warmth. It found a pile of pancakes on the table which Lena had baked for Robert. And the squirrel hung all these pancakes to dry around the house. It did it just like it hung mushrooms on the tree branches. Now the pancakes were hanging everywhere: on the sofa, on the rack in the hall, on the chairs ... When Robert came home the squirrel became frightened and hid. Robert saw that everything in the house was covered with pancakes ... And there was a note on the table from Lena: «Honey, this is for you.»

13

Eine Tolle Party

Ein sehr betrunkenes Mädchen, Laura Brown, wurde spät nachts auf die Polizeistation gebracht. Sie war wegen Trunkenheit am Steuer verhaftet worden. Sie konnte kaum aufrecht stehen. David war entsetzt als er sich vorstellte, wie sie in dem Zustand Auto fuhr.

«Du hattest vielleicht Glück, dass du verhaftet wurdest», sagte er zu Laura. «Denn es hätte dir etwas viel Schlimmeres passieren können.»
«Nein, sicher nicht,» erwiderte sie irritiert.
Sie war schlecht gelaunt. Natürlich wollte Laura nicht die ganze Nacht auf der Polizeistation verbringen. Es wurde schnell Morgen und sie bekam Kopfschmerzen. Laura rief ihre Freundin Kate an und bat sie, zu kommen und die Kaution zu hinterlegen. Kate stimmte zu.
«Und geh unterwegs in eine Apotheke, bitte,» sagte Laura zu ihr. «Ich habe schreckliche Kopfschmerzen nach all den Cocktails.»
«Nun, ist alles in Ordnung?» fragte David als

An Amazing party

Late at night a very drunk girl, Laura Brown, was brought to the police station. She was detained for drunk driving. She could barely stand on her own feet. David was terrified when he imagined how she was driving in such state.
«Perhaps you are lucky that you were detained», he said to Laura. «Because something much worse could have happened.»
«It could not,» she replied irritably.
She was in a bad mood. Of course, Laura did not want to spend the whole night at the police station. The morning was coming soon and she began to have a headache. Laura called her friend Kate and asked her to come and post bail for her. Kate agreed.
«And drop by a pharmacy on your way, please,» Laura told her. «I have a terrible headache after these cocktails.»
«Well, is everything all right?» David asked her when Laura hung up the phone.

sie auflegte.

«Ja, alles ist okay,» sagte Laura. «Meine Freundin kommt bald mit der Kaution und ich werde nach Hause gehen.»

«Es ist toll, so gute Freunde zu haben,» sagte David. «Nicht jeder ist bereit, aufzustehen und zur Polizei zu gehen wenn man ihn mitten in der Nacht aufweckt».

«Ich habe sie nicht aufgeweckt. Warum denken Sie das?» Laura war erstaunt. «Wir waren beide auf dieser tollen Party. Kate war auch gerade nach Hause gekommen, allerdings per Taxi.»

«Auf der tollen Party?» sagte David nachdenklich. Die Tatsache beunruhigte ihn, auch wenn er nicht verstand, warum.

Doch er fand bald heraus, dass seine Wachsamkeit nicht umsonst war. Eine Viertelstunde später erschien Kate auf der Polizeistation. Sie war genauso betrunken wie ihre Freundin Laura, aber sie kam nicht im Taxi. Ein Polizeiwagen brachte sie! Laura beobachtete verblüfft, wie die Polizisten Kate durch den Gang führten und in eine andere Zelle steckten.

«Deine Freundin hat in der Apotheke eine Packung Medizin genommen, aber ‚vergessen' zu bezahlen,» erklärte ihr der Polizist. «Und hier ist sie nun!»

«Naja, du hast mich gebeten, in die Apotheke zu gehen,» sagte Kate, die kaum stehen konnte.

«Oh nein,» sagte Laura traurig. «Nun müssen wir bis zum Morgen hier sitzen ... Und ich habe diese schlimmen Kopfschmerzen...»

«Versucht, jemand anderen anzurufen, der die Kaution übernimmt,» riet David ihnen. «Aber wählt jemanden, der nicht mit euch auf dieser tollen Party war!»

«Yes, everything is Okay,» Laura said. *«My friend will soon come with the bail and I will go back home.»*

«It's great to have such good friends,» David said. *«Not everyone is ready to get up and to go to the police when he is awakened in the middle of the night».*

«I did not wake her up. Why do you think so?» Laura was surprised. *«We were both with her at that amazing party. Kate had just returned home too, though she took a cab.»*

«At the amazing party?» David said thoughtfully. He became concerned about that fact, although he did not understand why.

Yet soon he found that his alertness was not vain. In a quarter of an hour Kate arrived at the Police station. She was drunk to the same extent as her friend Laura, but she did not come by taxi. She was brought in a police car! Laura watched in amazement when the policemen led Kate through the hall and then placed her in another cell.

«Your friend took a full package of medicine from the pharmacy, but she «forgot» to pay for it»- the policeman explained to her. *«And here she is now!'*

«Well, you asked to drop by the pharmacy,» Kate said, barely able to stand.

«Oh, no,» Laura said sadly. *«So, we have to sit here until morning ... And I also have this horrible headache ...»*

«Try to call someone else for the bail,» David advised them. *«But pick someone who has not been with you at that awesome party!»*

14

Eine Mysteriöse Stimme

Die Kinder spielten den ganzen Sommer über draußen und manchmal gingen sie zu einigen alten Scheunen. Kaum einer benutzte diese alten Scheunen. Die Erwachsenen waren sehr selten dort. Deshalb mochten die Kinder den Ort sehr. Aber einmal hörten sie eine leise Stimme aus einer Scheune. Sie gingen näher heran und die Stimme verklang. Dann klopften sie ans Scheunentor. Und hörten sofort eine heisere, ältliche Stimme:
«Bring die Knöpfe! Schneller!» rief die Stimme. Die Kinder bekamen Angst und liefen weg. Doch sie konnten nicht mehr spielen. Sie fühlten sich nicht mehr sicher.
«Wir haben ihm die Knöpfe nicht gebracht, « sagte ein Junge zu seinen Freunden. «Was, wenn uns etwas passiert?» fragte er. Keiner antwortete. Alle hatten Angst. Es wurde Abend und sie hatten noch mehr Angst. Die Kinder beschlossen, Knöpfe zur Scheune zu bringen. Sie wagten es nicht, noch mal zu klopfen. Sie schoben die Knöpfe einfach

A Mysterious Voice

The children played outside all summer, and sometimes they went to some old barns. Almost no one used these old bars. The adults were there very seldom. That is why the children liked the place very much. But once they heard a quiet voice from one of the barns. They came closer and this voice faded away. Then they knocked on the door. And immediately they heard a hoarse elderly voice:
«Bring the buttons! Faster!» The voice shouted.
The children were very frightened and ran away. But they could not play any more. They did not feel safe.
«We did not bring him the buttons,» one boy said to his friends. «What if something happens to us?» He asked. No one answered. Everyone was scared.
The evening was approaching and they were even more scared. The children decided to bring buttons to the barn. They did not dare to knock again. They just shoved the buttons

durch den Spalt unter dem Scheunentor, doch die Stimme beruhigte sich nicht.
«Ich will mehr Knöpfe!» rief er durch das Tor. «Bringt die Knöpfe! Und schneller!»
Er klang sehr ominös. Die Kinder brachten wieder und wieder Knöpfe aber es half nicht. Die Stimme wurde einschüchternder und verlangte erneut Knöpfe.
«Aber was sollen wir jetzt tun? Wir haben keine Knöpfe mehr,» flüsterten die Kinder. «Wo können wir welche finden?»
Dann beschloss eines der Kinder, nach Hause zu gehen und im Nähkasten der Mutter nach Knöpfen zu suchen, aber seine Mutter sah ihn.
«Also,» sagte sie. «Was ist hier los?»
Der Junge musste seiner Mutter von der Stimme und den Knöpfen berichten. Die Mutter runzelte die Stirn und ging zu dem Nachbarn, dem die Scheune gehörte. Dieser Nachbar war Davids Ehefrau Anna. Ein paar Minuten später gingen Anna, die Mutter des Jungen und die anderen Kinder zur mysteriösen Scheune. Die Kinder klopften an das Tor und die schreckliche alte Stimme war wieder zu hören:
«Ich will mehr Knöpfe!»
«Da ist nichts Schreckliches,» sagte Ann und öffnete das Scheunentor.
Sie machte das Licht an und alle sahen einen riesigen, wunderschönen Papagei!
«Er mochte nie im Käfig sitzen,» erklärte Anna, «und ich hatte für zwei Tage eine Katze bei mir. Meine Freundin fuhr für eine Weile weg und bat mich, für ihre Katze zu sorgen, also musste ich den Papagei hierher bringen,» sagte Anna.
Die Kinder sahen den Papagei erstaunt an. Konnte es sein, dass er sie derart ängstigte!
«Übrigens spielt er gerne mit Knöpfen» sagte Anna lächelnd. «Ihr habt sie also aus gutem Grund gebracht!» «Bringt die Knöpfe! Schneller!» rief der Papagei wieder und schaute die Kinder an.

into the crack under the door of the barn, but the voice did not calm down.
«I want more buttons!» He shouted through the door. «Bring the buttons! And do it faster!»
He sounded very ominous. The children brought buttons again and again but it did not help. The voice became more frightening and it demanded buttons again.
«But what should we do? We have no more buttons,» children were whispered. «Where can we find them?»
Then one of the kids decided to go home and search for buttons in his mother's sewing box, but his mother saw him doing this.
«Well,» she said. «What is going on here?»
The boy had to tell his mom about the voice and the buttons. Frowning, his mom went to the neighbor who owned the barn. This neighbor was David's wife Anna. A few minutes later Anna, the boy's mother and the other children went to the mysterious barn. Children knocked on the door and the terrible old voice was heard again:
«I want more buttons!»
«There is nothing terrible,» Anna said and opened the door of the shed.
She turned on the light and everyone saw there a huge beautiful parrot!
«It never liked to sit in a cage and it was always flying around the apartment,» Anna explained, «and I was given a cat for two days. My friend left for some time and asked me to take care of the cat, so I had to bring the parrot here for a while,» Anna said.
The children looked at the parrot with surprise. Can it be true that it could scare them so much!
«By the way, he likes to play with buttons» Anna said with a smile. «So you brought them here for a good reason!»
«Bring the buttons! Faster!» The parrot shouted again, looking at the children.

15

Eine Seltsame Gruppe

Einmal hatte David Nachtdienst mit seinem Partner. An dem Abend fand ein Football-Spiel statt, daher war die Nacht nicht besonders ruhig. Obwohl nichts Ungewöhnliches geschah, war die Polizei wachsam. David wurde sofort aufmerksam als er eine Gruppe betrunkener Männer sah. Es waren etwa fünfzehn Kerle und sie waren sehr laut. David hielt sie auf.
«Es ist schon mitten in der Nacht,» sagte er zu ihnen, «und da solltet ihr euch im Wohngebiet leise verhalten,» sagte David.
«Okay, wir werden leise sein», sagte ein Typ aus der Gruppe. «Die Party lief so gut, wir vergaßen wie spät es ist.»
David beschloss, ihre Papiere zu prüfen. Er sah sich den Ausweis des ersten Typen an und es war alles in Ordnung. Er checkte den Ausweis des zweiten Typen und auch da war alles okay, bis auf ein Detail. Der Name und

A Strange Group

Once David was on night duty with his partner. A football match was held that night, so the night was not very quiet. Although nothing unusual happened, the police were vigilant. David became immediately alert when he saw a group of drunken guys. There were about fifteen guys and they were very noisy. David stopped them.
«It's the dead of night already,» he told them, «and you should be quiet in a residential area in the middle of the night,» David said.
«Okay, we'll be quiet», one guy from the group replied. «The party went so well that we forgot what time it is.»
The rest of them laughed loudly and nodded. It seemed that the party went really well and even more then that.
David decided to check their documents. He checked the first guy's documents and everything was fine. He checked the second

Nachname des zweiten Typen war identisch mit dem Namen des ersten Mannes!
David sah sie verwirrt an. Sie sahen nicht aus als wären sie verwandt. Er begann, die restlichen Ausweise der Männer zu prüfen und sie überraschten ihn noch mehr. Er sah sich den dritten, vierten, fünften Ausweis an und es war dieselbe Geschichte.
Alle fünfzehn Personen hatten denselben Vor- und Nachnamen! David war geschockt. Die Betrunkenen kicherten leise und stießen sich mit den Ellbogen an. In dem Moment entschied David, dass es ernst war. Es sah aus wie Dokumentenfälschung! Und er war soweit, Verstärkung anzufordern, doch in dem Moment stoppte ihn einer der Männer.
«Uns scheint, als haben unsere Ausweise Sie überrascht, stimmt es?» sagte er.
«Keine große Sache. Es ist mein Job, mich mit allen möglichen überraschenden Dingen zu befassen», sagte David. «Und jetzt müssen wir das hier klären.»
Die Typen lachten wieder.
«Sehen Sie», sagte einer von ihnen, «es ist so, wir haben den Club der Namensvettern gegründet. Und wir kommen gerade von einem Clubtreffen. Und wir treffen Sie hier. Also sind alle Ausweise echt!» erklärte er.
David erkannte, er brauchte keine Verstärkung anfordern. Er wünschte ihnen eine gute Nacht und bat sie noch mal, leise zu sein. Ein Mann der Gruppe gab ihm seine Visitenkarte.
«Vielleicht haben Sie mal jemanden mit dem gleichen Namen getroffen?» fragte er. «Wir öffnen unseren Club für alle Namensvettern. Aber nur wenn die Ausweise echt sind!»

guy's documents and everything was fine too, except one detail. The name and the surname of the second guy was exactly the same as the first guy's!
David looked at them in confusion. They did not look like relatives at all. He began to check the rest guys' documents and they surprised him even more. He checked the third, the fourth, the fifth documents and it was the same story. All fifteen people had the same name and the same surname! David was in shock. Drunken guys giggled silently and nudged each other with their elbows. At that moment David decided that it was serious. It looked like a forgery of documents! And he was already about to call for backup but at that moment one of the guys stopped him.
«It seems to us that you are surprised at our documents, aren't you?» He said.
«It's no big deal. It is my job to deal with all sorts of surprising things.» David said. «And now we have to figure that out.»
The guys laughed again.
«Do you see», one of them said, «the fact is that we created the club of namesakes. And now we are just going from a meeting of the club. And here we met you. So all the documents are real!» He explained.
David realized that he has no need to call the backup. He wished them good night and asked to be quiet one more time. One guy from the group handed him his business card.
«Maybe you've met someone else with the same name?» He asked. «We initiate to our club all the namesakes. But only with real documents!»

Ein Wissenschaftliches Experiment

Lena liebte Tiere sehr. Sie war an allem interessiert, das mit Tieren zu tun hat. Einmal beschloss Robert, seine Frau positiv zu überraschen. Er hatte einem Biologieprofessor einen großen Dienst erwiesen, der seine Arbeit betraf. Dieser Professor studierte das Verhalten von Affen. Und Robert arrangierte, dass Lena eines seiner Experimente besuchen durfte. Lena war natürlich überglücklich! Sie hatte davon geträumt, bei einem echten wissenschaftlichen Experiment mit Affen anwesend zu sein. Am vereinbarten Tag traf sie den Professor in der Universität. Der Professor begrüßte sie freundlich.
«Ich habe eine ganze Reihe Experimente geplant,» sagte er. «Und Sie kommen zum ersten,» sagte er zu Lena. «Ich bin Ihnen so dankbar!» erwiderte Lena. «Es interessiert mich wahnsinnig!»

A Science Experiment

Lena loved animals very much. She was interested in everything that concerned them. Once Robert decided to make his wife a pleasant surprise. He rendered one professor of biology a great service concerning his work. This professor studied the behavior of monkeys. And Robert arranged that he allow Lena to visit one of his experiments.
Of course, Lena was overjoyed! She dreamed to be present at a real scientific experiment with monkeys. On the appointed day she met with the professor at the university. The professor greeted her in a friendly way.
«I planned a whole series of experiments,» he said. «And you came to the very first,» he told Lena.
«I am so grateful to you!» Lena answered. «I'm awfully interested!»

Das Ziel des Experimentes war es, das Verhalten von Schimpansen unter verschiedenen Umständen zu testen. Das Experiment fand in einem abgeschiedenen, sauberen Raum statt. Es gab eine Menge verschiedenes Spielzeug: Puppen, Bälle, Spielzeugautos, Bausätze, Stofftiere... Der Professor brachte den Schimpansen in das Zimmer und schloss die Tür.
«Ich will studieren, wie er sich in Abgeschiedenheit verhält», erklärte der Professor Lena. «Ich habe die Tür absichtlich geschlossen. Der Schimpanse muss nicht wissen, dass er beobachtet wird. So wird sein Verhalten natürlich sein.»
«Was glauben Sie, welches Spielzeug wird er als erstes nehmen?» flüsterte Lena nach einer Weile.
«Das werden wir jetzt sehen», sagte der Professor.
Er lehnte sich leise vor und schaute in ein spezielles Fenster in der Tür. Aber nach einem Moment richtete er sich auf und hatte einen verwirrten Gesichtsausdruck.
«Was ist los?» fragte Lena.
«Sehen Sie selbst,» sagte der Professor zu ihr. Lena beugte sich zum Fenster in der Tür und sah, dass die braunen Augen des Schimpansen sie ansahen. Er beobachtete interessiert, was die Leute da machten.

The aim of the experiment was to study the behavior of chimpanzees in different circumstances. The experiment took place in an isolated clean room. There were a lot of different toys: dolls, balls, toy cars, erector sets, stuffed toys... The professor brought the chimpanzee into the room and closed the door.
«I want to study how it will behave in a solitude», the professor explained to Lena. «I closed the door intentionally. The chimpanzee does not have to know that it is being watched. In this case its behavior will be natural.»
«How do you think what toy he will take the first?» Lena whispered after a while.
«We'll see now», the professor said.
He quietly leaned and looked into a special window in the door. But in a moment he straightened up and his face was bewildered.
«What is it?» Lena asked.
«Look for yourself,» the professor told her. Lena leaned to the window in the door and saw that the chimpanzee's brown eye was looking at her from there. It watched with interest what the people were doing there.

17

Ein Unvorhersehbares Detail

Als Vincent und Julia bereit waren, einen Laden auszurauben, hatten sie einen guten Plan. Sie waren über sieben Jahre verheiratet und das bedeutete, sie verließen sich in allem aufeinander. Der Plan war einfach und sie dachten, er würde sicher funktionieren. Vincent musste den Raub durchführen und leise alles stehlen, worauf sie sich geeinigt hatten. Julias Aufgabe war, ihn zu decken. Sie musste die Sicherheitsleute beobachten und ablenken. Sie dachten nach und entschieden, im Fall einer Gefahr würde Julia ... sich ausziehen. Währenddessen konnte Vincent in Ruhe mit den gestohlenen Dingen hinaus schleichen.
Am Tag des Raubüberfalls versuchte Vincent, sich so unauffällig wie möglich zu kleiden, aber es war schwer, nicht auf Julia aufmerksam zu werden. Sie sah bezaubernd aus! Sie betraten den Laden nicht zusammen, sondern

An Unforeseeable Detail

When Vincent and Julia were about to rob a store they had a good plan. They had been married for more than seven years and that is why they relied upon each other in everything. The plan was simple and they thought that it would surely work. Vincent had to rob and quietly steal everything that they had agreed upon. Julia's responsibilities were to cover for him. She had to watch the guards and distract them. They thought and decided that in a case of danger Julia would ... undress. Meanwhile Vincent could calmly sneak out of the store with the stolen goods.
On the day of the robbery, Vincent tried to dress as unnoticeably as possible, but it was hard not to notice Julia. She looked charming! They entered the shop not together but at a five minute interval, so no one could think that they are together.

mit fünf Minuten Abstand, damit niemand auf den Gedanken kam, dass sie ein Paar waren. Zu Beginn lief alles gut. Julia ging gemächlich im Laden umher und tat, als würde sie nur auswählen, was sie haben wollte; und aus dem Augenwinkel beobachtete sie das Sicherheitspersonal und sah ruhig zu, was Vincent tat.

Alles verlief perfekt.

Durch Zufall ging Robert in denselben Laden um ein Geschenk für seine Frau zu kaufen. Eine ungewöhnliche Szene erregte seine Aufmerksamkeit. Als die Sicherheitsleute ihre Runden drehten und dabei ans andere Ende des Ladens kamen, begann eine hübsche Frau in Rot plötzlich damit, sich langsam auszuziehen. Die Sicherheitsleute erstarrten ob der Überraschung. Robert erstarrte auch und betrachtete ihr schamloses Verhalten. Einen Moment lang schauten sie nur auf das, was da geschah. Dann kam einer der Sicherheitsleute zur Besinnung.

«Also, hören Sie zu,» murmelte er. «Sie sind in der Öffentlichkeit. Was Sie tun ist verboten.»
Doch die Frau erklärte nichts und sprach kein Wort. Sie lächelte still und zog sich weiter aus. Das Sicherheitspersonal vergaß ganz, was sie tun wollten. Sie waren verwirrt. «Bitte ziehen Sie sich an,» versuchten sie sie zu überreden. «Oder wir müssen...» sagte einer von ihnen. Aber er redete etwas unschlüssig.
«Siehst du nicht, dass der Frau heiß ist,» unterbrach ihn ein anderer Sicherheitsbeamter. «Machen Sie es sich nur bequem,» fügte er an die Frau gewandt hinzu.

Alle waren so vertieft in das Geschehen, dass keiner Vincent bemerkte. Der war da bereits bei der Tür und trug ruhig alle Dinge, die er brauchte, hinaus. Er war nur noch ein paar Schritte von seinem Erfolg entfernt. Aber dann machte Vincent einen Fehler – er schaute zurück zu seiner Frau.

Und ihr Auftritt schockierte ihn! Seine Frau stand fast nackt in der Mitte des Ladens, umgeben vom Sicherheitspersonal und

At the beginning everything was going well. Julia leisurely walked around the store pretending that she was just choosing what she wanted, and out of the corner of her eye she watched the guards and looked quietly at what Vincent was doing. Everything was going perfectly.

By chance Robert came to the same store too. He came to buy a gift for his wife. His attention was attracted by an unusual scene. When the guards were on their rounds and went to the other end of the store a beautiful woman in red suddenly began to undress slowly. The guards froze because of such a surprise. Robert froze also looking at her brazen behavior. For a moment they were just looking at what was happening. Then one of the guards came to his senses.

«Well, listen,» he mumbled. «You are in a public place. It is forbidden».

But the woman did not explain anything and did not say a word. She smiled silently and continued to undress. The guards have completely forgotten what they were about to do. They were confused.

«Please, get dressed,» they tried to persuade her. «Or we'll have to...» One of the guards said. But he spoke a little bit irresolutely.

«Don't you see that the woman feels hot,» another guard interrupted him. «Go ahead and make yourself comfortable,» he added, addressing the woman.

They were all so absorbed with what was happening that no one noticed Vincent. And at the same time he was already at the door and quietly carried out all the things he needed from the store. Just a few steps were left for him to succeed. But then Vincent made a mistake - he looked back at his wife. And he was shocked with the performance! His wife was standing in the middle of the store almost naked and she was surrounded by security guards and other visitors, many of whom were men. Vincent could not stand

Kunden, viele davon Männer. Vincent ertrug es nicht! Vor Eifersucht schmiss er alle gestohlenen Dinge auf den Boden, eilte zu seiner Frau und warf seine Jacke auf sie. Das Geräusch der gestohlenen Dinge, die zu Boden fielen, brachte die Sicherheitsleute zur Besinnung.
Robert erkannte sofort, was da abging, genauso wie die Sicherheitsbeamten. Sie verhafteten das Ehepaar sofort, noch bevor die Polizei eintraf.

it! He threw all the stolen things on the floor because of his jealousy and rushed to his wife to fling his jacket on her. The noise produced by the stolen things fallen to the floor made the guards come to their senses. Robert immediately realized what was happening as well as the guards. They immediately arrested both spouses before the arrival of the police.

18

Aberglauben

Gabys Schwiegermutter wurde im Alter immer abergläubischer. Oma hatte schon lange an Horoskope geglaubt und alle waren daran gewöhnt. Doch dann fing sie an zu glauben, dass schwarze Katzen Unglück bringen, dass keiner einen Spiegel zerbrechen darf, und so weiter. Manchmal besuchte sie ihre Freundin, die durch Kartenlesen die Zukunft voraussagte. Und natürlich glaubte die ältliche Frau alles, was die Wahrsagerin ihr sagte, auch wenn es totaler Unsinn war. Eines morgens läutete jemand an der Haustür obwohl niemand erwartet wurde. Vormittags war Gabys Schwiegermutter allein im Haus. Sie öffnete die Tür und sah eine grausliche, verlumpte alte Frau dort stehen, die wie eine echte Hexe aussah.
«Was wollen Sie?» fragte Gabys Schwiegermutter. «Geben Sie eine Spende, sonst passiert das, was in Hamptonville geschah, hier!» - sagte die alte Frau mit unheilvoller Stimme. «Und dort ist etwas Schreckliches passiert,» fügte sie drohend

Superstitions

With age, Gaby's mother-in-law became more and more superstitious. The granny has believed in horoscopes for a long time already and everyone was used to it. But then she began to believe that black cats bring misfortune, that one can not break the mirror and so on. Sometimes she visited her friend who told fortune by reading cards. And of course, the old woman believed everything that the fortuneteller told her even if it was absolute nonsense.
Then one morning someone rang the doorbell, even though no one was expected to come. In the morning Gaby's mother-in-low stayed home alone. She opened the door and saw a horrible, ragged old woman on the threshold. She looked like a real witch.
«What do you need?» Asked Gaby's mother-in-law.
«Make a donation, otherwise the thing that happened in Hamptonville will happen here!» - the old woman said with ominous voice.
«And something terrible happened there,» she added threateningly.

hinzu.
Ihr graues Haar wehte in der Brise. Schwiegermutter bekam Angst und gab ihr etwas Geld. Sie war erleichtert als der ungebetene Gast ging. Aber am nächsten Morgen wiederholte sich das Ganze.
«Hören Sie zu,» Schwiegermutter runzelte die Stirn. «Sie waren gestern schon hier. Es reicht.»
Aber es schien als hörte die Frau sie nicht. Sie schaute geradeaus ohne mit den Augen zu blinzeln und wirkte sehr furchteinflößend.
«Spenden Sie an die armen Menschen. Sonst geschieht das, was in Hamptonville passiert ist, hier!» sagte sie unheilvoll.
Schwiegermutter war ängstlich und gab ihr wieder Geld. Das ging einige Tage so. Doch dann erkältete Gaby sich plötzlich und blieb mit Schwiegermama zuhause. Gaby war sehr erstaunt als sie morgens die Türklingel hörte. Doch sie war noch erstaunter als sie das Gespräch zwischen ihrer Schwiegermutter und der Hexe hörte. «Oh, Sie schon wieder», sagte Schwiegermutter hilflos.
«Ich bin wegen der Spende hier. Geben Sie mir Geld. Sonst passiert das, was in Hamptonville geschah, auch hier,» sagte die alte Frau mit drohender Stimme.
Schwiegermutter war wieder ängstlich und griff nach ihrer Geldbörse. Gaby gefiel das natürlich überhaupt nicht!
«Einen Moment,» sagte Gaby zu der alten Frau. «Was ist in Hamptonville passiert?»
Die alte Frau seufzte.
«Oh, etwas Schreckliches, Grausames ist dort passiert! In Hamptonville habe ich gar nichts bekommen.»

Her gray hair waved in the breeze. The mother-in-law was scared and gave her some money. She felt relieved when uninvited guest left. But the next morning the same thing happened again.
«Listen,» the mother in law frowned. «You came here yesterday. It's enough.»
But it seemed that the woman heard nothing. She looked straight ahead with unblinking eyes, and looked very scary.
«Donate to the poor. Otherwise the thing that happened in Hamptonville will happen here!» She said ominously.
The mother-in-law was nervous and gave her money again. This continued for several days. But suddenly Gaby caught a cold and stayed at home with her mother-in-law. Gaby was very surprised to hear the doorbell ring in the morning. But she was even more surprised when she heard the dialogue between her mother-in-law and the witch.
«Oh, it's you again», the mother-in-law said helplessly.
«I came for the donation. Give me some money. Otherwise the thing that happened in Hemptonville will happen here,» the old woman said in a threatening voice.
The mother-in-law was nervous again and reached out for her wallet. Of course, Gaby did not like that all!
«Wait a minute,» Gaby told the old woman. «What happened in Hamptonville?»
The old woman sighed.
«Oh, a terrible, horrible thing happened there! They gave me nothing in Hamptonville».

19

Gute Nachbarn

Eines Tages erhielt die Polizei eine etwas ungewöhnliche Beschwerde. Die Frau behauptete, dass ihr Nachbar ihr Haustelefon abhörte. Sie verlangte, dass sofort Maßnahmen eingeleitet wurden. David besuchte sie in ihrem Haus um herauszufinden, was wirklich vor sich ging.

Die Frau war sehr glücklich, dass David sie aufsuchte. Sie fing sofort an, sich bei ihm zu beschweren.

«Ich halte es nicht mehr aus!» sagte sie empört. «Warum bin ich so interessant für ihn? Er hört alle meine Telefongespräche ab!»

«Warum Sie sind Sie da so sicher?» fragte David. «Vielleicht bilden Sie es sich nur ein?»

«Oh nein!» sagte sie. «Erstens weiß er immer über meine Angelegenheiten Bescheid. Und es ist oft so, dass ein Fremder nichts darüber wissen kann. Aber da ist noch mehr! Manchmal höre ich ihn sogar leise kichern.»

«Aber warum glauben Sie, er ist derjenige?»

Good Neighbors

One day the police received a not very common complaint. The woman claimed that her neighbor wiretapped her home phone. She demanded to take measures immediately.

David went to her place to find out what was really going on.

The woman was very happy that he came. She began to complain to him immediately.

«I can't stand it any more!» she said indignantly. «Why am I so interesting for him? He listens in to all my phone calls!»

«Why are you so sure about this?» David asked. «Maybe it's just your imagination?»

«Oh no!» she said. «First of all he is always aware about all my affairs. And it is often so that a stranger could not know about these affairs. But more than that! Sometimes I can even hear him giggling softly.»

«But why do you think it's him?» David was surprised. «Maybe it's someone else

David war überrascht. «Vielleicht kichert da jemand anderes?»
«Nein, ich kenne sein Kichern. Glauben Sie mir,» sagte die Frau selbstbewußt. «Keiner außer ihm hat ein so fieses Kichern. Ich habe es lange toleriert, aber jetzt reicht es! Sie müssen ihn verhaften,» sagte sie zu David.
David dachte einen Moment nach.
«Ja, ich sehe, es ist ernst. Sieht so aus als haben Sie recht,» sagte er. «Ich muss Verstärkung anfordern. Kann ich Ihr Telefon benutzen?»
«Ja, klar, bitte machen Sie,» sagte die Frau.
David rief auf der Polizeistation an.
«Hallo, Harry? Schick mir das SWAT Team,» sagte David. «Sieht so aus als hat die Frau recht. Der Nachbar hört ihr Telefon ab. Wir müssen eingreifen. Sie sagt, sie erkennt ihn an seinem fiesen Gekicher im Telefonhörer. Wir müssen den Schurken festnehmen. Okay, wir warten!» sagte David und legte auf.
«Werden Sie ihn verhaften?» fragte die Frau hoffnungsvoll.
«Ich glaube schon. Verstärkung ist unterwegs», bestätigte David.
Nur ein paar Minuten später läutete es an der Tür.
«Können die so schnell hier sein,» die Frau war erstaunt und ging um die Tür zu öffnen.
Aber es war nicht die Polizei. Ihr Nachbar stand auf der Türschwelle. Er war ganz rot vor Entrüstung.
«Hören Sie, ich bin ein ehrlicher Mann!» sagte er ohne überhaupt Hallo zu sagen. «Diese Frau lügt! Wie können Sie so etwas denken – dass ich Ihre Gespräche abhöre? Und ich habe kein fieses Kichern, ist das klar? Ich kichere überhaupt nicht!» rief er.
«Ja, vermutlich,» stimmte David zu. «Wie auch immer, als Sie mein Gespräch mit der Polizeistation abhörten, haben Sie anscheinend nicht gekichert», sagte David mit einem Lächeln.
Natürlich wurde der glücklose Spion bestraft.

giggling?»
«No, I know his giggle. Believe me,» the woman said confidently. «No one has such a nasty giggle except him. I tolerated it for a long time, but now it's enough! You have to arrest him,» she told David.
David thought for a moment.
«Yes, I see that it is a serious matter. It looks like you are right,» he said. «I will have to call back up. Can I use your phone?»
«Yes, sure, please,» the woman said.
David dialed the police station.
«Hello, Harry? Send to me the SWAT team,» David said. «It looks like this woman is right. The neighbor wiretaps her phone. We must take measures. She says she recognized him by his nasty giggling in the telephone receiver. We'll have to arrest the villain. Okay, we are waiting!» David said and hung up.
«Are you going to arrest him?» The woman asked hopefully.
«I think so. The backup is on its way,» David confirmed.
Just a few minutes later the doorbell rang.
«Could they have come so quickly,» the woman was surprised and went to open the door.
But it was not the police. Her neighbor stood on the threshold. He was all red with indignation.
«Listen, I'm an honest man!» he said without even saying hello. «This woman is just lying! How could you think about such a thing - that I wiretap your conversations? And my giggling is not nasty, is that clear? I do not giggle at all!» he shouted.
«Yes, probably,» David agreed with him. «In any case, when you taped my conversation with the police station, it seems that you didn't giggle,» David said with a smile.
Of course, the unlucky spy was punished.

20

Ein Ruheloser Patient

Als Christian gesundheitliche Probleme hatte, fand David eine gute Klinik für seinen Vater. Und Christian musste ein paar Tage dort verbringen. Ein alter Mann kam in seine Abteilung. Er war schon über 90 Jahre alt. Er verließ sein Bett fast nie und hatte Probleme mit seinem Gedächtnis. Opa war freundlich und lächelte viel. Aber Christian ging es nicht gut und deshalb redete er kaum mit ihm. Abends langweilte Opa sich. Er drückte den Rufknopf und die Krankenschwester kam. Opa bat sie um etwas Wasser. Die Schwester erfüllte seine Bitte. Er dankte ihr herzlich und sie kehrte auf die Station zurück. Aber weniger als fünf Minuten später drückte Opa den Rufknopf erneut. Die Schwester erschien wieder. Opa sah sie einen Moment lang an ohne etwas zu sagen.
«Nun, wie ist das Wetter?» fragte er schließlich.
«Ist es nicht heiß?»

A Restless Patient

When Christian had some health problems, David found a good health clinic for his father. It happened so that Christian had to spend a few days there. One old man was put in the ward with him. He was already more then 90 years old. He almost didn't get up from bed and he had some problems with his memory. Granddad was friendly and smiled a lot. But Christian did not feel well and that is why he almost did not speak with him.
In the evening the grandfather felt bored. He pushed the call button and the nurse came. Granddad asked to give him some water. The nurse agreed to his request. He thanked her warmly and she returned to her post. But in less than five minutes the granddad pushed the call button again. The nurse came again. Grandpa looked at her for a moment without saying anything.
«Well, how is the weather now?» He finally asked. «Isn't it hot?»

«Nein, es ist nicht heiß,» erwiderte die Schwester, «das Wetter ist super.»
«Und es ist nicht windig?» fragte Opa.
«Der Wind ist sehr schwach. Kein Regen in der heutigen Vorhersage», sagte die Schwester.
Sie unterhielten sich etwas über das Wetter, dann ging sie. Nach ein paar Minuten rief Opa sie erneut. Christian war verärgert weil dauernd jemand ins Zimmer kam. Er konnte nicht schlafen.
«Brauchen Sie etwas?» fragte die Schwester den Opa.
«Nein», sagte er. «Ich brauche nichts. Wissen Sie, morgen kommt mich meine Enkelin besuchen. Sie ist so klug!» Und sie sprachen etwa fünf Minuten lang über seine Enkelin. Die Schwester führte die Unterhaltung höflich fort, doch schließlich sagte sie, sie müsse auf ihren Posten zurückkehren, denn die anderen Patienten könnten sie brauchen. Aber nach zehn Minuten drückte Opa wieder den Rufknopf und die Schwester kam erneut. Opa fragte sie nach den Besuchszeiten der Klinik. Die Schwester erklärte sie ihm ausführlich. Er dankte ihr und sie ging. Aber er rief sie bald wieder.
Die Schwester erschien wieder.
«Brauchen Sie wieder etwas?» fragte die Schwester. Opa dachte eine Weile nach.
«Nein, nichts,» sagte er. «Übrigens, sagen Sie... Ich habe diesen Knopf mehrmals gedrückt... Wofür ist der?»

«No, it's not,» the nurse replied, «the weather is great.»
«And there is no wind?» the granddad asked.
«The wind is very weak. The rain was not in forecast for today,» the nurse said.
They talked a little bit about the weather and she left. A few minutes later the granddad called her again. Christian was annoyed that somebody was walking into the ward all the time. It didn't let him sleep.
«Do you need something?» the nurse asked the granddad.
«No», he said. «I don't need anything. You know, tomorrow my granddaughter will come to visit me. She is so clever!» And he talked about his granddaughter for about five minutes.
The nurse politely kept up the conversation but after all she said that she had to get back to her post. Because the other patients might need her.
But in ten minutes the granddad pushed the call button again and the nurse came again. The granddad asked her when visitation was allowed in the clinic. The nurse explained everything in detail. He thanked her and she left. But soon he called her again.
The nurse came again.
«Do you need something again?» the nurse asked.
The granddad thought for a while.
«No, nothing,» he said. «And by the way, tell me ... I pushed this button several times ... And what is it for?»

21

Ein Vorfall am See

Während einer seiner Schichten musste David in einem mysteriösen Fall am See ermitteln. Er bemerkte sofort, dass die Umstände dieses Falles merkwürdig waren. Deshalb rief David Robert an und bat diesen, mitzukommen. Robert willigte ein.
Ein sehr aufgebrachter Mann wartete auf sie in der Nähe des Sees. Er erklärte, dass er und seine Frau eine Bootfahrt auf dem See machten. Plötzlich fiel seine Frau ins Wasser und ertrank.
«Ich habe sofort die Polizei gerufen,» sagte er. Er war so aufgeregt, er konnte sich kaum auf den Beinen halten. Er nahm einen Schluck Brandy aus einem Flachmann um sich zu sammeln.
«Sie ist ertrunken und Sie haben uns sofort gerufen?» fragte David.
«Ja, genauso war es,» sagte der Mann.
«Und sie haben nicht mal versucht, sie zu retten?» fragte David.
«Ich kann nicht schwimmen,» sagte der Mann und er begann zu weinen. Sein Kummer schien echt zu sein.
David schaute zweifelnd auf das Boot und zum

An Incident by the Lake

During one of David's shifts he had to investigate a mysterious case by the lake. He immediately noticed that the circumstances of the case were strange. That is why David called Robert and asked him to go with him. Robert agreed.
A very upset man was waiting for them near the lake. He explained that he and his wife went boating on the lake. Suddenly his wife fell overboard and drowned.
«I called the police immediately,» he said. He was so upset that he could hardly stand on his feet. He took a gulp of brandy from a flask in order to come to senses.
«She drowned and you called us immediately?» David asked.
«Yes, that's how it was,» the man said.
«And you did not even try to rescue her?» David asked.
«I cannot swim,» the man said and began to cry. His grief seemed sincere.
David looked doubtfully at the boat and at the lake. It was not too deep though it was deep enough to drown.
«It is very strange that she fell overboard,»

See. Er war nicht allzu tief, aber tief genug um ertrinken zu können.

«Es ist sehr seltsam, dass sie aus dem Boot fiel», sagte Robert. «Erzählen Sie uns genau, wie es passiert ist.»

Der Mann zuckte mit den Schultern.

«Ich weiß es nicht. Ich ruderte und sie fiel ins Wasser und ertrank. Das ist so schrecklich!» sagte er und fing wieder an zu weinen.

In dem Augenblick läutete das Handy des Mannes. Der unglückliche Mann suchte lange in all seinen Taschen danach und konnte sich nicht erinnern, wo es war. Schließlich fand er es und starrte begriffsstutzig auf das Display. Robert kam näher um zu sehen wer es war. Seine Frau rief an!

David nahm das Handy und sagte er würde antworten. Der Mann war total verwirrt. David stellte sich vor und fragte, wer anrief.

«Oh Gott!» rief die Frau am anderen Telefon. «Ich bin Alex' Frau. Sie sind von der Polizei? Was ist ihm zugestoßen? Lebt er?»

«Ja, er lebt,» sagte David. «Aber er ist nicht sicher, was Sie angeht.»

«Was meinen Sie damit?» die Frau war überrascht. «Ich verstehe Sie nicht. Alex ging am Nachmittag aus dem Haus. Er sagte, er würde eine Bootfahrt auf dem See unternehmen. Jetzt ist es schon Nacht und er ist noch nicht zuhause. Ich habe mir schon Sorgen gemacht! Also, was ist mit ihm?» fragte sie.

«Es scheint als hatte er einen schönen Bootsausflug,» sagte David und schaute zu dem Mann. Dieser nahm wieder einen Schluck Brandy aus dem Flachmann. David erkannte plötzlich, dass dieser Alex nicht vor Kummer kaum stehen konnte; er war einfach nur sturzbetrunken!

David konnte sich nur wundern warum ihnen das nicht von Anfang an aufgefallen war.

«Bitte schicken Sie ihn nach Hause!» bat die Frau.

«Alkohol und ein unnötiger Anruf bei der Polizei... Ich fürchte, wir werden ihn erstmal in eine Zelle sperren müssen,» sagte David.

Robert said. «Tell us in detail how this happened.»

The man shrugged his shoulders.

«I do not know. I was rowing and she fell overboard. And drowned. It's so awful!» He said and began to cry again.

At this moment the man's phone rang. The unhappy man looked for it in all his pockets for a long time and could not remember where it was. Finally, he found it and stared at the screen with a dull expression. Robert came closer to see who it was. His wife was calling!

David took his phone and said that he would answer. The man was completely confused. David introduced himself and asked who was calling.

«Oh, God!» The woman on the phone cried. «I am Alex's wife. So are you from the police? What happened to him? Is he alive?»

«Yes, he is alive,» David said. «But he is not sure about you».

«What do you mean?» the woman was surprised. «I do not understand you. Alex left this afternoon. He said that he would go boating on the lake. It's night already and he is not home yet. I began to worry already! So what happened to him?» she asked.

«It seems that his boating trip went well,» David said looking at the man.

He took a gulp of brandy from a flask again. David suddenly realized that this Alex could hardly stand not because of grief. He was just blind drunk! David could only wonder how they hadn't noticed it at the beginning.

«Please send him home!» The woman asked.

«Alcoholism and an unnecessary call for the police... I'm afraid that we have to put him in a cell for now,» David said.

22

Eine Kaffee-Garantie

Robert wurde mit der Untersuchung eines interessanten Falles beauftragt. Er musste einige Zeugen befragen. George, der erste auf der Liste, arbeitete im Technischen Support. Am Telefon sagte er, dass er bereit war, Roberts Fragen zu beantworten und er bat Robert, zu seiner Arbeitsstelle zu kommen. Um keine Zeit zu verlieren, ging Robert noch am selben Tag zu ihm. George spendierte ihm einen Kaffee und bereitete sich vor, zu antworten.
«Sagen Sie mir,» begann Robert.
Doch dann läutete das Telefon. George nahm das Gespräch an und hörte dem Anrufer zu.
«Es tut mir leid, aber ich muss mit einer Kundin sprechen,» sagte er eine Minute später zu Robert. «Unsere Manager konnten ihre Frage nicht beantworten. Ich muss den Anruf annehmen.»
Robert sagte er würde warten. Das Telefon war auf Lautsprecher gestellt, und so konnte Robert die Kundin deutlich hören.

54

A Coffee Guarantee

Robert was assigned the investigation of one interesting case. He had to question some witnesses. George who was the first on the list worked in technical support. Over the phone he said that he was ready to answer Robert's questions and asked Robert to come to his workplace. In order not to lose time Robert came to see him the same day. George treated him to coffee and prepared to respond.
«Tell me,» Robert began.
But then the telephone rang. George picked up the phone and listened to the person on the line.
«I'm sorry but I have to talk to a client,» he said to Robert a minute later. «Our managers could not answer her question. I would have to take the call.»
Robert said that he would wait. The phone was set to the speaker, so Robert could hear the client very well.
«You see,» she said, «the coffee holder was

«Sehen Sie,» sagte sie, «der Kaffeetassenhalter an meinem Computer brach ab. Und der Computer hat noch Garantie und deshalb möchte ich ihn kostenfrei gegen einen neuen austauschen.»
«Hmm, ein Kaffeetassenhalter?» erwiderte George erstaunt. «Ich erinnere mich nicht an ein solches Modell. Haben Sie den Computer mit Kaffeetassenhalter bestimmt in unserem Geschäft gekauft?»
«Ja, natürlich,» sagte sie. «Ich habe alle Unterlagen.»
«Interessant…» wunderte George sich. «Haben Sie das Modell während eines Sonderverkaufes erstanden?»
«Nein, habe ich nicht,» sagte sie.
«Hmm,» wiederholte George. «Also, dann beschreiben Sie, wo sich der Halter befindet.»
«Nun, auf dieser… Systemeinheit,» erklärte das Mädchen.
«Ich verstehe gar nichts,» zuckte George mit den Schultern. «Welcher Kaffeetassenhalter … Ich glaube nicht, dass wir so etwas verkaufen. Sagen Sie mir, steht da etwas drauf?»
«Warten Sie eine Minute, ich sehe nach» – sagte das Mädchen. «Nichts wie es aussieht. Oh, nein, da steht, 32 X.»
«32 X?» fragte George.
«Ja, genau» - sagte sie.
Robert brach in Lachen aus und sah George an, der auch lächelte. Natürlich begriffen beide, dass sie ihren Kaffeebecher auf den CD-ROM-Einschub gestellt hatte …

broken down on my computer. And the computer is still under warranty that is why I want to exchange for a new one for free.
«Hmm, a coffee holder?» George replied in surprise. «I don't remember such a model. Did you buy the computer with a coffee holder in our shop for sure?»
«Yes, of course,» she said. «I have all the documents.»
«It's interesting…» George wondered. «Did you buy this model on some sale?»
«No, I did not,» she said.
«Hmm,» George repeated. «Well, then describe where this holder is situated».
«Well, on this… system unit,» the girl explained.
«I don't understand anything,» George shrugged his shoulders. «What coffee holder … It seems to me that we did not sell anything like that. Tell me, is there something written on it?»
«Wait a minute, I'll take a look now» - the girl said. «It seems like nothing. Oh, no, it says, 32 X.»
«32 X?» George asked.
«Yes, exactly» - she said.
Robert burst out with laughter looking at George who smiled too. Of course, they both realized that she put her coffee on the drawer of the CD-ROM …

Ein Zotteliger Partner

Quentin hatte schon einige Raubüberfälle verübt, daher war er sicher, dieses Mal würde alles gut gehen. Er war fast überhaupt nicht nervös. Aber sein Hund Gina war in letzter Zeit immer nervös. Immer wenn sie alleine zuhause war fing sie an, laut zu heulen. Die Nachbarn beschwerten sich über ihr Gebell. Und die letzten Male als keiner zuhause war, ruinierte Gina die Möbel und die Situation strapazierte auch die Nerven von Quentins Frau. Wie das Pech es wollte, konnte am Tag des Überfalls keiner den Hund nehmen. Quentin vermutete, dass aufgrund des Hundegeheuls alle Nachbarn herausfinden würden, dass keiner zuhause war. Er glaubte nicht, dass jemand sie fragen würde – dazu würde es wohl nicht kommen. Trotzdem wollte er nicht, dass die Nachbarn mitbekamen, wann genau er ging und zurückkam. Das war heute völlig unnötig. Nach kurzem Zögern entschied er, Gina mitzunehmen. Sie konnte in den fünf

A Shaggy Partner

Quentin has commit robberies before, so he was sure that this time everything would go well. He was almost not nervous at all. But recently his dog Gina became nervous. She began to howl loudly whenever she stayed home alone. Neighbors complained that she howled. And the last few times when no one was home Gina spoiled the furniture badly and Quentin's wife's nerves were also frayed. As ill luck would have it, on the day of the robbery there was no one to leave the dog with. Quentin figured that all the neighbors would find out that no one was home because of the dog's howling. He did not think that someone would ask them - it was unlikely that it would come to that. But still he did not want the neighbors to know to the exact minute when he left and when he came back. Today it was completely unnecessary. After a moment's hesitation he decided to take Gina with him. She could howl as much as she wanted during those five minutes which he

Minuten, in denen er in der Bank war, soviel heulen wie sie wollte; denn auf einer lauten Hauptstraße würde keiner auf sie achten.
Wie er erwartet hatte, lief der Raubüberfall wie ein Uhrwerk ab. Quentin war glücklich, dass er alles so gut geplant hatte. Doch als er die Autotür öffnete, sprang Gina sofort aus dem Auto!
Den ganzen Morgen hatte er den Raubüberfall vorbereitet und ganz vergessen, dass seine Frau ihn gebeten hatte, mit Gina hinaus zu gehen. Und jetzt verrichtete sie ihr Geschäft am nächsten Baum. Die Welt verfluchend beschloss Quentin, eine halbe Minute auf den Hund zu warten.
Aber als Gina sich vom Baum abwandte, entschied sie, ein bißchen herumzulaufen. Der Zeitpunkt passte überhaupt nicht! Quentin versuchte, sie einzufangen aber das klappte nicht. Er hörte die Polizeisirenen.
Es war Zeit zu fliehen. Es tat ihm leid, Gina zurückzulassen. Aber was konnte er tun? Quentin stieg ins Auto und fuhr weg. Als die Polizei ankam war es zu spät. Quentin war bereits weit entfernt.
David, der am Ort des Verbrechens eintraf beschloss, die Zeugen zu befragen. Eine alte Dame kam sofort auf ihn zu. Sie war klein, sah aber sehr resolut aus.
«Sehen Sie den Hund dort?» fragte sie David. «Ich glaube, dieser Hund gehört dem Räuber. Ich sage Ihnen, es ist so! Ich habe alles gesehen,» fügte sie stolz hinzu.
David interessierte ihre Aussage. Er kam immer gut mit Tieren aus und rief den Hund einfach zu sich. Sie wedelte freundlich mit dem Schwanz und ließ ihn ihr Ohr kraulen. Somit brauchte David nur die Adresse des Räubers auf dem Halsband lesen.

would spend in the bank, because no one will pay attention to her in a noisy main street.
As he expected, the robbery went like clockwork. Quentin was happy that he planned everything so well. But when he opened the car door Gina immediately jumped out of the car! All morning he had been preparing for the robbery and he completely forgot that his wife had asked him to take the dog for a walk. And now she was doing its business by the nearest tree.
Cursing everything in the world, Quentin decided to wait for the dog for half a minute. But when Gina left the tree alone she decided to run a little bit. It was not an appropriate time at all! Quentin tried to catch her but that didn't work out. He heard the police sirens. It was time to escape. He was sorry to leave Gina. But what could he do? Quentin got into the car and drove away. It was too late when police arrived. Quentin was already far away.
David, who arrived on the scene of the crime, decided to question the witnesses. One old lady immediately came up to him. She was small but had a very resolute look.
«Do you see that dog?» she asked David. «I think that this dog belongs to that robber. I'm telling you! I saw everything,» she added proudly.
David was interested in what she said. He always got along with animals and called the dog up easily. It wagged its tail in a friendly way and let him scratch its ear. So that David had only to read the address of the robber on its collar.

24

Die Beste Kaffeemaschine auf der Welt

Einmal bekam Anna einen Anruf von einer Firma, die Haushaltsgeräte verkaufte. Sie sagten, dass sie gerade sehr gute Kaffeemaschinen verkauften.
«Sie sollten Sie sich auf jeden Fall ansehen!» sagten sie zu ihr.
«Danke, aber ich habe schon eine Kaffeemaschine,» erwiderte Anna. «Aber die ist nicht wie unsere! Unsere Kaffeemaschinen sind viel besser!» wurde ihr versichert.
Anna erklärte, dass sie nichts kaufen würde, aber sie waren hartnäckig und versuchten fünf Minuten lang, sie zu überreden. Schließlich musste Anna auflegen. Sie musste schnell zur Arbeit und konnte nicht länger reden.
Doch zu ihrer Überraschung erhielt sie auf der Arbeit wieder einen Anruf von dieser Firma. Es war sehr unangenehm. Und als Anna abends nach Hause kam, riefen sie noch mal an und sprachen wieder über ihre Kaffeemaschinen. Ann wurde sehr sauer.
«Hören Sie, rufen Sie mich nicht mehr an,» sagte sie fest. «Ich brauche keine Kaffeemaschine.»
Das Mädchen am anderen Ende der Leitung

The Best Coffee-maker in the World

Once, Anna got a cal from a company that sold household appliances. They said that they were selling very good coffee-makers at the time.
«You should certainly see it!» they told her.
«Thanks, but I already have a coffee maker,» Anna replied.
«But this one is not like yours! Our coffee-makers are much better!» they assured her.
Anna explained that she was not going to buy anything, but they insisted and tried to persuade her for five minutes. Finally, Anna had to hang up. She was in a hurry to go to work and she could not talk.
But to her surprise she received a phone call at work from this firm again. Anna did not talk to them thought they called her back a few times. It was very unpleasant. And in the evening when Anna came home they called again and began to talk about their coffee-makers again. It made Anna terribly angry.
«Listen, stop calling me,» she said firmly. I do not need a coffee-maker.
The girl on the other end of the wire sighed sadly.

seufzte traurig. «Niemand braucht Kaffeemaschinen,» sagte sie bedrückt. «Und die Chefs sagen, ich mache meine Arbeit schlecht. Diese Woche hatte ich nicht eine einzige Heimpräsentation. Man wird mich entlassen!» jammerte sie.
«Ich fühle mit Ihnen,» sagte Anna. «Aber ich werde trotzdem nichts kaufen.»
«Nun, dann lassen Sie mich wenigstens zu Ihnen nach Hause kommen und eine Präsentation machen. Das kostet Sie gar nichts,» bat das Mädchen.
Anna gab unerwartet auf und stimmte zu. Am nächsten Tag hörten sich Anna und David über eine Stunde lang eine Präsentation über «die besten Kaffeemaschinen auf der Welt» an. Die Berater redeten und zeigten viel; sie erklärten ausführlich jede Funktion. Die Kaffeemaschine war wirklich sehr gut. Aber Anna war total zufrieden mit dem Kaffeeautomaten in ihrer Küche.
«Danke, es war sehr interessant,» sagte David ihnen endlich. «Aber wie wir schon sagten, wir brauchen keine Kaffeemaschine.»
Dann baten die Berater sie, ihnen die Telefonnummern von Leuten zu geben, die Interesse an ihren Kaffeeautomaten haben könnten. Sie deuteten an, dass sie dann nicht mehr anrufen würden. Anna dachte einen Moment nach. Natürlich wollte sie keine Nummer ihrer Freunde herausgeben, also gab sie ihnen die Nummer einer Kollegin, mit der sie oft stritt.
Die Beraterin schaute auf die Telefonnummer und sagte: «Nein, tut mir leid, nicht diese Person.»
«Warum nicht?» Anna war erstaunt.
«Weil sie es war, die Sie empfohlen hat,» sagte sie.

«Nobody needs coffee-makers,» she said sadly. *«And the authorities say that I work badly. This week I did not even have a single home presentation. I will be fired!»* She complained.
«I sympathize with you a lot,» Anna said. *«But I'm still not going to buy anything.»*
«Well, then let me at least come to your place and do a home presentation. It won't cost you anything,» the girl asked.
Unexpectedly, Anna gave up and agreed. The next day Anna and David listened to a presentation about «the best coffee-makers in the world» for more than an hour. The consultants talked and showed a lot; they explained every function in detail. The coffee-maker was really very good. But Anna was completely satisfied with the coffee-maker that stood in her kitchen.
«Thank you, it was very interesting,» David finally told them. *«But, as we said, we do not need a coffee-maker.»*
Then the consultants asked to give them the phone number of any person who may be interested in their coffee-makers. They hinted that in this case they will stop to call. Anna thought for a moment. Of course, she did not want to give them any of her friend's phone number, so she gave him a colleague's phone number with whom she often quarreled.
The consultant looked at the phone number and said:
«No, I'm sorry, but this person will not do».
«Why not?» Anna was surprised.
«Because she recommended you to us,» she said.

25

Wer Braucht es Mehr?

An dem Tag hatte David bei Gericht zu tun. Der Fall: Der Besitz eines Ehepaares sollte aufgeteilt werden. Er hielt es für einen langweiligen Routinefall, also hörte er nicht sehr aufmerksam zu und dachte an seine eigenen Angelegenheiten. Er hatte schon lange geplant, sich ein neues, teures Telefon zu kaufen, und an dem Abend wollten David und seine Frau es kaufen. David dachte weiter darüber nach, ob er eine gutes Modell gewählt hatte oder nicht. Dann gab es auf einmal eine Störung im Gerichtssaal. Der Richter gab die Entscheidung bekannt.
Er teilte den Besitz wie folgt auf: ein Bügeleisen, ein Staubsauger, ein Bett und ein Herd gingen an die Ehefrau; ein Kühlschrank, ein Fernseher und ein Sofa gingen an den Ehemann. Es gab keine Einwände. Doch ein anderer Punkt verursachte die Störung. Es ging um ein Telefon. «Es ist ein sehr teures Telefon und mein Mann kann es nicht haben!» sagte seine Frau.

Who Needs it More?

That day David was on duty at court. A case about the division of property of one couple was being conducted. The case seemed to him routine and boring so he did not listen very carefully and thought about his own matters. He had been planning to buy himself a new expensive telephone for a long time, and this evening David and his wife were going to buy it. David continued to think about whether he chose a good model or not. Then suddenly a disturbance began in the courtroom. The judge announced the decision.
He divided the property as follows: a flat-iron, a vacuum cleaner, a bed and a cooker went to the wife; a refrigerator, a TV and a sofa went to the husband. It did not cause any objections. But there was another point because of which the disturbance began. It was because of a telephone.
«It's a very expensive phone and I can't let my husband have it!» his wife said.
She began to explain in details that she

Sie fing an, detailliert zu erklären, dass sie das Telefon viel nötiger brauchte als ihr Mann. Ihr Mann wurde sehr ärgerlich als er zuhörte.

«Warte, das ist mein Telefon!» sagte er als er an der Reihe war. «Es hat mich fast die Hälfte meines Gehaltes gekostet! Selbstverständlich muss es an mich gehen!»

Er zog das Telefon aus seiner Hosentasche um allen zu zeigen, dass es ihm gehörte und es in seiner Tasche war.

«Nein, es gehört mir», warf die Ehefrau ein. «Du hast es heute morgen gestohlen!»

In dem Moment läutete das Telefon. Die Frau riss es ihrem Mann aus der Hand um sich zu melden. Ihr Mann war wütend und nahm es ihr aus der Hand. Er hatte sogar Zeit, «Hallo» zu sagen, doch dann schubste seine Frau ihn und er stürzte und das Telefon fiel auf den Boden. Seine Frau schnappte es sofort und rannte damit aus dem Gerichtssaal. Ihr Mann stand auf und lief ihr nach. David erkannte, es war Zeit einzugreifen. Er rannte auf die Straße, dem Paar hinterher um sie zu trennen. Als er auf sie zulief, hatte der Mann seine Frau gerade an den Haaren gepackt und sie biss ihn in die Hand. David trennte die beiden mit großer Mühe. Sie reagierten erst als er ihnen das Telefon wegnahm und sie bat, ins Gericht zurückzukehren. Der Richter schaute das Paar aufmerksam an und wandte sich dem Ehemann zu:

«Wenn Ihre Frau bereit ist, wegen dem Telefon so ein Risiko einzugehen, dann lassen Sie es ihr.» Der Ehemann wurde rot vor Zorn aber argumentieren war zwecklos. Der Fall wurde geschlossen und jeder verzog sich langsam.

David hatte bei seiner Arbeit schon viel gesehen, aber das heutige Ereignis beeindruckte ihn sehr. Er ging aus dem Gerichtssaal und rief als erstes seine Frau an.

«Nun, meine Liebe? Bist du bereit, einkaufen zu gehen?» fragte er.

«Sicher doch, ich warte nur auf dich!»

needed the telephone much more that her husband. Her husband became very angry, listening to all this.

«But wait, it is my telephone!» He said when it was his turn. «I paid for it almost half of my salary! Of course, it must stay with me!» He pulled the phone out of his pocket to show everyone that the telephone belonged to him and it was in his pocket.

«No, it is mine», the wife objected. «You just stole it this morning!»

At that moment the phone rang. The woman pulled it out of her husband's hand to answer the call. Her husband was angry and pulled the phone out of her hand. He even had time to say «hello» but then his wife pushed him and he fell and dropped the phone on the floor. His wife immediately grabbed the phone and ran out of the courtroom with it. Her husband got up and ran after her. David understood that it was time to intervene. He ran into the street after the couple to separate them.

When he ran up to them, the husband had just grasped the woman's hair and she was biting his hand. With great difficulty David separated them. They responded only when he took away the phone and asked them to return to court.

The judge looked at the couple attentively and addressed the husband:

«If your wife is ready to take a risk like that for the sake of the telephone then let her get it.»

The husband turned red with anger but it was useless to argue. The case was closed and everyone slowly began to disperse. David has seen a lot in his line of work, but today's event made a great impression on him. He walked out of the courtroom and first of all he called his wife.

«Well, my dear? Are you ready to go shopping?» he asked.

«Of course, I'm waiting for you!» she replied cheerfully.

erwiderte sie fröhlich.
David war eine Weile still.
«Weißt du was,» sagte er schließlich, «ich habe nachgedacht … Ich brauche das Telefon eigentlich nicht so sehr. Ich glaube, es wäre besser wenn wir es für dich kaufen.»
Seine Frau war sehr überrascht. «Das ist natürlich eine sehr unerwartete Entscheidung,» antwortete sie nach einer Pause. «Aber bleib ruhig dabei, ich werde nicht mit dir darüber streiten», lachte sie.

David was silent for a while.
«You know what,» he said at last, «I've been thinking … Actually, I don't need that telephone that much. I think it would be better if we buy it for you.»
His wife was very surprised.
«Of course, this is a very unexpected decision,» she replied after a pause. «But let it be, I'm not going to argue with you, she laughed.»

Ein Fataler Streit

Lena und Robert waren zu einer Hochzeit eingeladen. Lenas Freund Mary heiratete und hatte beide eingeladen. Zwei Wochen lang versuchte Lena, ein Kleid auszuwählen. Doch dann, ganz plötzlich und direkt vor dem Hochzeitstermin rief Mary Lena an und sagte, die Hochzeit war abgesagt.
«Wir stritten oft,» sagte Mary. «ich will jetzt nicht einmal mehr mit ihm reden.» Ihr Verlobter hatte sie sehr verärgert.
«Aber vielleicht ist die ganze Sache nicht so schlimm,» sagte Lena.
«Vielleicht versöhnst du dich wieder mit ihm.» Mary seufzte nur tief. Die Zeit verging, doch sie kamen nicht wieder zusammen. Mary sagte Lena, dass ihr Verlobter sie ständig anrief. Aber Mary ging nicht ans Telefon und ließ ihn nicht ins Haus als er kam. Er versuchte sehr, sich mit ihr zu versöhnen, doch sie wollte immer noch nicht mit ihm reden. Und dann hörten seine

A Fatal Quarrel

Lena and Robert were invited to a wedding. Lena's friend Mary was going to get married and invited them. Lena has been trying to choose a dress for two weeks. But suddenly, just before the wedding, Mary called Lena and said that the wedding is canceled.
«We quarreled a lot,» Mary said. «Now I don't even want to talk to him!» She was very offended by her fiancé.
«But maybe everything is not so bad,» Lena said. «Maybe you'll make it up with him.»
Mary just sighed heavily. Time went by but they did not reconcile. Mary told Lena that her fiancé called her all the time. But Mary did not pick up the phone and did not let him in when he came. He tried to make up hard but she still did not want to talk to him. And suddenly his calls stopped. Mary

Anrufe plötzlich auf. Mary war sehr aufgebracht, da sie bereit gewesen war, ihre Meinung zu ändern. Aber er rief nicht an und kam auch nicht zu ihr. Es herrschte komplette Funkstille.
«Also, ruf du ihn an,» versuchte Lena, sie zu überreden. «Er rief dich an und hat sich so oft entschuldigt.»
«Nein, ich kann nicht anrufen,» antwortete Mary stur. «Vielleicht bin ich zu stolz ...»
Weitere drei Monate vergingen und es gab keine Versöhnung. Und dann erhielt Mary eines Tages einen Umschlag per Post. Es war eine Einladung zur Hochzeit ihres Ex-Verlobten! Mary fand den ganzen Tag keine Ruhe und sie war sehr deprimiert. Sie konnte an nichts anderes denken. Sie wanderte nur ziellos von einer Ecke zur anderen. Am Abend ging sie zu Lena um ihr ihren Kummer anzuvertrauen. Mary war total am Boden.
«Stell dir das vor!» sagte sie zu Lena. «Wie konnte er mich so schnell vergessen! Schließlich wollte ich ihn heiraten!» meinte sie frustriert.
«Ja, das ist schon furchtbar,» sagte Lena. «Aber hör mal zu, warum öffnen wir nicht den Umschlag? Es wäre schon noch interessant zu wissen, wer seine Braut ist.»
«Nein, es interessiert mich nicht,» sagte Mary ernst.
«Obwohl, doch! Ich muss es wissen!» änderte sie auf einmal ihre Meinung. Mary nahm den Umschlag mit der Einladung aus ihrer Handtasche und öffnete ihn. Und sie sah neben dem Namen des Bräutigams ihren eigenen Namen...

was very upset because she was ready to change her mind. But he did not call and did not come. There was complete silence.
«Well, call him yourself,» Lena tried to persuade her «He called you and apologized so many times».
«No, I cannot call myself,» Mary replied stubbornly. «Perhaps I'm too proud ...»
Another three months passed and they did not reconcile. And then one day Mary received an envelope by mail. It was an invitation to the wedding of her ex-fiancé! Mary could find no peace anywhere all day long and she was terribly depressed. She could not think about anything else. She just walked aimlessly from one corner to another. In the evening she went to Lena to share her grief. Mary was completely crushed.
«Just imagine!» she told Lena. «How could he forget me so quickly! After all I was going to marry him!» she said in frustration.
«Yes, indeed, it's awful,» Lena said. «But listen, why don't we open the envelope? It is still interesting to know who his bride is».
«No, I'm not interested,» Mary said sternly. «Although, yes! I have to know that!» Suddenly she changed her mind. Mary took the envelope with the invitation from her purse and opened it. And she saw that the next to the groom's name there was her own name...

27

Ein Guter Alter Freund

Dieses Mal kam die Polizei sofort zur überfallenen Bank und der Täter hatte so gut wie keine Chance zu entkommen. Polizisten waren an mehreren Häuserblöcken in der Umgebung postiert und alle Straßen waren gesperrt. Die Polizei arbeitete sehr schnell und allen war klar, dass der Täter noch in der Nähe war. Er konnte schließlich nicht weit kommen. Um die Wahrheit zu sagen, er trug eine Maske als er die Bank überfiel und das komplizierte den Fall. David stand bei einem der Posten und sah jeden Passanten und jedes vorbeifahrende Auto aufmerksam an. Plötzlich sah er eine Person deren Gesicht ihm bekannt vorkam. Es war sein alter Freund. Er und David waren zusammen im selben Football-Team gewesen. David lächelte als er ihn sah. Ein fröhliches Treffen mit einem alten Freund gerade jetzt war eine große

An Old Good Friend

This time the police came to the robbed bank immediately, and the perpetrator had almost no chance of escape. Police posts were set on several blocks around there, and all the roads were blocked. The police worked very quickly, and everyone understood that the perpetrator was still nearby. After all, he just couldn't get far. To tell the truth, he robbed the bank in a mask and it complicated the whole case. David stood on one of the posts and watched every passer-by and every passing car attentively. Suddenly he saw a person whose face seemed familiar to him. It was his old friend. He and David used to play together on the same football team. David smiled when he saw him. A cheerful meeting with a good old friend was a big surprise at such a moment. David kindly waved his hand and his friend

Überraschung. David winkte ihm freundlich zu und sein Freund sah ihn auch. Er hob seine Hand und erwiderte Davids Winken. Dann verflog Davids gute Stimmung sofort. Die Hand seines Freundes hatte Flecken aus fluoreszierender Farbe.
Dasselbe Farbmittel wurde für den Schutz von Bank-Geldkassetten benutzt. David erkannte, das Treffen würde sich nicht auf eine freundliche Begrüßung beschränken. Er flüsterte seinem Partner ein paar Worte zu und rief seinem Freund zu, näher zu kommen. Der war sicherlich nicht begeistert darüber, doch er tat es um keinen Verdacht zu erregen. Inzwischen umrundeten die Polizisten sie leise.
«Hallo, alter Bursche,» sagte David traurig zu ihm. Es tat ihm sehr leid, dass sein alter Freund sich auf Banküberfälle verlegt hatte.
«Nun ja, das ist sehr unerwartet,» erwiderte sein Freund und sah sich um. «Wir haben uns lange nicht gesehen!»
«Ja, du hast recht,» sagte David, «um der alten Zeiten willen biete ich dir Wasser und Seife an um die Bankfarbe von deinen Händen zu waschen. Ich kann dir auch eine gemütliche, saubere Zelle anbieten.»
Die Gesichtsfarbe von Davids Freund wechselte sofort. Er merkte, er war von Polizisten umgeben.
«Aus irgendeinem Grund habe ich keinen Zweifel, dass er dein nettes Angebot annehmen wird!» sagte Davids Partner mit einem Lächeln.

saw him too. In response he also waved his hand to David. Then David's good mood vanished instantly. His friend's hand was stained with fluorescent dye.
The same dye that they use for the protection of bank boxes with money. David understood that this meeting would not be limited to a friendly greeting. He whispered a few words to his partner and called his friend to come closer. He was certainly not eager to do it, but still he agreed in order not to arouse any suspicions. Meanwhile, the policemen were quietly surrounding them.
«Hello, old chap,» David told him sadly. He was very sorry that his old friend resorted to bank robbery.
«Well yes, it is so unexpected,» his friend replied looking around. «Long time no see!»
«Yes, you are right,» David said, «For old times' sake, I can offer you some water and soap to wash your hands from the banking dye. I can also offer you a comfortable clean cell.»
David's friend immediately changed color. He noticed that he was surrounded by police.
«For some reason, I have no doubt that he will take your friendly offer!» David's partner said with a smile.

28

Maulwürfe - Musikliebhaber

David und Anna waren sehr glücklich als sie ein Landhaus kauften. Sie wollten schon sehr lange so ein Haus weit weg vom Stadtlärm haben. Sie renovierten Einiges und richteten das Haus perfekt ein. Aber mit einer Sache hatten sie kein Glück. Es gab ein Problem mit Maulwürfen. Diese lebten direkt auf Davids Grundstück. Die Maulwürfe gruben den ganzen Hof um und sorgten dafür, dass Annas Blumenbeete erbärmlich aussahen. David und Anna stolperten ständig über die Maulwurfshügel. Natürlich gefiel ihnen das gar nicht. Sie versuchten alles um die Maulwürfe loszuwerden! Aber es stellte sich heraus, dass die Tiere erstaunlich robust waren. David versuchte ein Dutzend verschiedene Dinge mit ihnen, aber die dreisten Tiere waren unbezwingbar. Sie lebten weiter im Hof und gruben ihre Hügel überall. Anna und David waren entsetzt. Sie wussten nicht, was sie tun sollten. Zu der Zeit hatten ihre Nachbarn Besuch von ihrem Neffen. Ein Teenager, etwa

Moles - Music Lovers

When David and Anna bought a cottage they were very happy. They had wanted to have such house far away from the city hubbub for a very long time already. They made some renovations and furnished the house perfectly. But they had no luck with one thing. There was a problem with moles. They lived right on David's property. Moles dug over the whole yard. Anna's flowerbeds looked miserable because of them. David and Anna tripped on their burrows all the time. Of course, they did not like it at all. They tried everything to exterminate the moles! But the animals turned out to be surprisingly resilient. David tried a dozen of different means on them but the cheeky animals were invincible. They continued to live in the yard and they dug their burrows everywhere. Anna and David were horrified. They did not know what to do. At this time, a nephew came to visit their

dreizehn Jahre alt. Er hörte von dem Problem und schlug eine ungewöhnliche Lösung vor. «Diese Methode wirkt sogar bei den fiesesten Nachbarn,» verriet der Junge ihnen mit einem Lächeln. «Maulwürfe werden ihr sicher nicht standhalten.»

Die Methode war folgende. Der Junge bot an, in der Mitte des Hofes zwei große, tiefe Löcher zu graben. Dann brachte er riesige Musik-Lautsprecher von zuhause. Sie setzten die Lautsprecher in die Löcher und verbanden sie mit Stromkabel. Sobald es Nacht wurde, schaltete der Junge Hardrockmusik in voller Lautstärke ein. Es war natürlich nicht nur für die Maulwürfe eine harte Nacht. Doch David und Anna ertrugen alles tapfer um ihre unterirdischen Bewohner loszuwerden.

In der vergangenen Nacht ebneten sie den Boden im Hof. Und am nächsten Morgen stellten sie glücklich fest, dass es nicht einen einziges neues Loch bzw. Hügel gab. Die Methode funktionierte! Um das Ergebnis zu verbessern, fanden die Hardrock-Konzerte für die Maulwürfe einige weitere Nächte statt. Und es war wunderbar – der Hof war immer noch ohne Löcher und Hügel. Die Maulwürfe hatten sie endlich verlassen! David und Anna waren fast daran gewöhnt, mit lauter Musik zu schlafen. Doch eines Tages wachten sie früh morgens auf weil es ungewöhnlich still war. David machte sich daran, herauszufinden was passiert war. Die Antwort war einfach... Die Maulwürfe hatten in der Nacht das unterirdische Elektrokabel zernagt. Und in der Hofmitte waren neue Maulwurfshügel zu sehen...

neighbors. He was a teenager about thirteen years old. He heard about their problem and proposed an unusual solution. «This method is good even for the nastiest neighbors,» the boy told them with a smile. «Moles will not withstand it for sure.»
The method was as follows. The boy offered to dig two large deep holes in the middle of the yard. Then he brought huge loudspeakers for music from home. They placed these loudspeakers into the holes and connected them to electricity. As soon as night came the boy turned on hard rock in top volume. Of course, it was a difficult night not only for the moles. But David and Anna bravely endured everything in order to get rid of the underground inhabitants. The previous night they leveled the ground in the yard. And they were very happy to see that the next morning there was not a single new hole or heap. The method worked! To improve the result they arranged the hard rock concerts for the moles several nights more.
And it was wonderful - the yard was still without holes and heaps. Finally the moles left them! David and Anna became almost used to sleeping with loud music. But suddenly one day they woke up early in the morning because of an unusual silence. David began to find out what happened. The answer was simple ... It turned out that at night the moles gnawed the electric wire underground. And new burrows could be seen in the middle of the yard...

29

Kriminalpsychologie

David und Robert machten ab, am Abend in eine Kneipe zu gehen. Doch David wurde von einer unerwarteten Sache aufgehalten. In einem Fachgeschäft für Elektroartikel wurde ein großer Raubüberfall verübt und David fuhr zum Ort des Verbrechens. Robert beschloss, ihn dort abzuholen und gleichzeitig zu sehen, was passiert war.
«Kannst du dir das vorstellen? Sie haben das Glas eingeschlagen und die Fernsehgeräte direkt aus dem Schaufenster gestohlen», sagte David zu Robert als der eintraf.
Robert untersuchte den Laden genau.
«Was ist dein Plan?» fragte er.
«Wir werden in dem Fall wie üblich ermitteln,» antwortete David. «Jetzt gehen wir mit dir in die Kneipe. Ich bin hier bereits fertig.»
Robert schüttelte den Kopf.
«Ich denke, du hast schon oft gehört, dass der Verbrecher immer an den Tatort zurückkehrt. Ich glaube, wir sollten uns hier verstecken und auf sie warten,» schlug er vor.
«Nein», sagte David. «Wäre es so einfach, dann gäbe es nichts zu ermitteln. Wir würden nur am Tatort sitzen und warten bis die Verbrecher

Psychology of the Criminal

David and Robert agreed to go to a pub in the evening. But David was detained by the unexpected affair. A huge robbery was committed in an electronics store and David went to the scene of the crime. Robert decided to pick him up right there and at the same time to have a look what happened.
«Can you imagine? They broke the glass and stole TV- sets right from shop-window,» David said to Robert when he arrived.
Robert examined the store carefully.
«What you plan to do?» he asked.
«We will investigate the case as usual,» he answered. «We'll go with you to the pub now. I have already finished here».
Robert shook his head.
«I think you have heard a lot of times already that the criminal always returns to the scene of the crime. I believe that we should hide here and wait for them,» he suggested.
«No», David said. «If it were that easy, we would have nothing to investigate. We

zurückkommen,» lachte er.
Aber Robert meinte es ernst.
«Vertrau meiner Intuition,» sagte er. «Heute könnte es so ein Fall sein. Sie könnten zurückkommen.»
David war sich da nicht so sicher aber er stimmte Robert zu. Sie beschlossen, die Nacht über zusammen zu bleiben und zu warten.
Ein paar Stunden lang geschah nichts. David bereute insgeheim, dass er und Robert nicht in die Kneipe gegangen waren, denn dort machte es abends mehr Spaß als in einem dunklen Laden zu sitzen ...
Plötzlich hörten sie ein leises Geräusch. Die Polizisten warteten bis die Besucher in den Laden kamen und schlossen dann vorsichtig die Tür. Die Räuber hatten nicht erwartet, jemanden anzutreffen. Deshalb waren sie verwirrt als sie die Polizisten sahen. Sie wurden sofort gefasst.
Robert machte das Licht an und sah sie mit einem zufriedenen Lächeln an.
«Ich habe dir gesagt, sie werden zurückkommen,» sagte er und zeigte David ein Päckchen, dass die Räuber fallen gelassen hatten. Es enthielt etwas, wofür sie zurückgekommen waren. Das erste Mal nahmen sie nur die Fernseh-Sets aus dem Schaufenster. Darum kamen sie nun zurück, wie Robert vermutet hatte, um die dazugehörenden Fernbedienungen zu holen.

would just sit at the scene of the crime and wait until the criminals come back,» he laughed.
But Robert was serious.
«Trust my intuition,» he said. «It may be such a case today. They can come back here.»
David was not sure about this but he agreed with Robert. They decided to stay together for the night and wait.
Nothing happened for a few hours. David secretly regretted that he and Robert did not go to the pub, since it's more fun there at night than in the dark shop ...
Suddenly they heard a quiet noise. The policemen waited until the guests came into the shop and carefully closed the door. The robbers did not expect to meet anyone there. That is why they were confused when they saw the policemen. They were immediately seized.
Robert turned on the light and looked at them with a satisfied smile.
«I told you that they would be back,» he said and then showed David a package which was dropped by the robbers. It was something for which they came back. The first time they took only the TV-sets from the shop-window. That is why they came back now, as Robert suspected, to take the remote controls for them.

Buchtipps

Second German Reader
Bilingual for Speakers of English
Pre-Intermediate Level
by Elisabeth May
Audio tracks are available on lppbooks.com free of charge

Discover the Power of the ALARM Method

Second German Readers is a Beginner and Pre-Intermediate level graded reader to learn German language easier and faster. If you already have background with German language, this book is the best one to try. It makes use of the so-called ALARM or Approved Learning Automatic Remembering Method to efficiently teach its reader German words, sentences and dialogues. Through this method, a person will be able to enhance his or her ability to remember the words that has been incorporated into consequent sentences from time to time. By practicing this method, German can be learned in a fun and convenient way. You will

learn German vocabulary without hassle with parallel English translation. Audio tracks available on the publisher's homepage free of charge will teach you German pronunciation. You will have fun learning German through this book because you will comprehend everything. You will be able to understand and create German dialogues as well. Second German Reader is ultimately comprehensive because each chapter is created with words explained in previous ones and with as few as possible new words. The author of this book used every opportunity to use the words used in the previous chapters to explain the succeeding chapter. This way, the reader will be able to understand every single detail of the book. Learning through this Second German Reader is like attending a sophisticated step-by-step lecture of Pre-Intermediate level. There is also First German Reader for complete beginners that was made in the same way. Those who do not have any background about German should start with First German Reader before moving on to Second German Reader.

* * *

Made in the USA
Middletown, DE
11 October 2015